Choice Awar
Logotherapy &
Treatment of Add...

By Pavel G. Somov, Ph.D.

Foreword by
Marie S. Dezelic, Ph.D., Diplomate in Logotherapy

Choice Awareness: Logotherapy and Mindfulness Training for Treatment of Addictions

Copyright © 2008 by Pavel Somov/I-Catching Books

Table of Contents

Modern psychology has not paid much attention to how much complicated action may be performed automatically.
Ellen J. Langer (Mindfulness, 1989)

The book introduces a tri-partite change equation consisting of the following three change variables: freedom-to-change, reason-to-change, and method-to-change. The freedom-to-change construct is conceptually differentiated from the construct of self-efficacy, and is operationalized through Choice Awareness Training.

Choice Awareness Training, which involves a combination of Logotherapy and modified Mindfulness training, is introduced as an element of the overall clinical curriculum for substance use and compulsive spectrum clinical presentations. The book reviews a curriculum of discussions and exercises designed to challenge cognitive- behavioral automaticity and freedom-restricting belief schemas that constitute phenomenological barriers to one's perceived freedom-to- change.

The book concludes with a sample of qualitative evaluative data from client participants obtained from a 2002-2003 pilot of Choice Awareness Training in the context of a residential, correctional drug and alcohol treatment program in an American jail (Allegheny County Jail, Pittsburgh, PA).

Foreword

Marie S. Dezelic, Ph.D., Diplomate in Logotherapy

Quest for Recovery: Discovering the Answer that Lies Within You

What is unique about this book, and why this book over any other for addictions recovery treatment? One provocative and powerful word... FREEDOM. Freedom opens up an entirely new dimension, full of avenues out of the treacherous hold of the addiction cycle, disease model, and recovery that never lasts. But *what* exactly is freedom, and how do we uncover access to freedom when we feel we are stuck, have no choices, have a disease, have our minds and bodies controlled by an outside force or substance, or simply cannot see a way out? And *is* freedom actually enough to change a global epidemic, an immense population of people across the continents, irrespective of age, gender, culture, color, creed, circumstance, location, and socio-economics, who have become addicted to a substance or behavior for which an entire industry of medical professionals, mental-health therapists, treatment centers of every type, and psychopharmacology, has been developed around fixing, helping, supporting and recovering? The answer is an astounding yes! *Freedom* is the missing link in the quest for recovery, and this ordinary word lies and lives within you with extraordinary potentials.

Dr. Pavel Somov takes us through his innovative Recovery Approach that is founded upon a matter-of-fact and potent "Change Equation." He brilliantly bridges Existential-Humanistic theory (third wave psychology) with Mindfulness practice and training (eastern contemplative traditions) to offer a realistic and tangible path toward not only substance recovery, but for change in any area of our lives. Viktor Frankl's Logotherapy & Existential Analysis, known as the "Third Viennese School of Psychotherapy" after Sigmund Freud's Psychoanalysis and Alfred Adler's Individual Psychology, is a meaning-centered psychotherapy and philosophy built upon the notion that *Will to Meaning* is the thriving and motivating factor in human existence; it views the human being as comprised of three inseparable dimensions of mind, body, and spirit (the existential essence, the core of uniqueness of the individual). It is within the spiritual dimension, (from a non-religious stance) in the core of our being-ness and alive-ness, that we have a *Will to Meaning, Meaning in Life,* and *"Freedom" of Will*—the "freedom to" take a stand toward human conditions and change our attitude in the face of difficulties, limitations, suffering, pain, and setbacks, not "freedom from" the conditions of life. This freedom is the unique element of change, or the change-agent that human beings posses as an inner resource continuously available to us.

Somov blends Logotherapy & Existential Analysis philosophy and methods from his own Mindfulness practices and teachings to bring us to an awakened mind, awareness of our existential freedom as human beings, and a process to make lasting changes. The "Change Equation" focuses on: (1) a *Reason-to-Change*—the internal meaning-motivation to achieve a desired goal, (2) a *Method-to-Change*—the skillset (or "skillpower" as Somov has called it) to make ongoing and lasting changes by handling uncomfortable situations, emotionally challenging or physiological responses, and (3) the *Freedom-to-Change*—the existential, inner resource within our core being that we have to engage in order to find ourselves able, capable, and unrestricted of automaticity and vicious mindless patterns of behaviors. These three concise elements added together can lead to exponential results and the change that we desire.

Freedom opens the door to *Choices*. When we are enslaved, choice is limited, and our agency thwarted. When our *Attitude* begins to shift, and we open to the awareness of recognizing we are free and not pre-determined beings, even within life's conditions and limitations, suddenly choices present themselves; we can make conscious decisions to take new stands, make new choices, and thereby experience new outcomes. Freedom directly links to Choices.

The three simple, yet profound elements to the "Change Equation" coupled with the innovative "Choice Awareness Training" methodology, revolutionizes recovery treatment and the process of addictions. Moving away from the disease model of addictions, toward enlightening individuals with our freedom to choose, responsibility to our individual existence, awareness of choices, and capacity to change, this book offers clinicians a format to follow in addressing some of the most difficult and challenging questions, and assumptions made in addictions therapy.

Choice Awareness Training focuses on (1) developing a strategic awareness of the freedom to change, (2) a reformulation or rethinking of the perceived automaticity of addiction and loss of personal control, and (3) the development of a tactical awareness of the freedom to change, through guided experiential and mindfulness exercises. To understand addiction concepts is helpful in recovery—knowing the "why" behind our behaviors, but to have a felt-sense, embodied experience (existential know-how) of our often mindless autopilot states, and how we give in to or give up our ability to make conscious choices, allows us to capture the concepts and make lasting changes—learning the "how" to change our behaviors through a personal existential awareness. In my "Meaning-Action Triangle," I have conceptualized three parts of a triangle, (1) *Noticing,* becoming conscious, (2) *Responsibility,* the existential owning of one's life and choices, and (3) *Take Action,* the freedom to make new choices, that will then lead toward uncovering V. Frankl's Meaning Triangle of *Creativity, Experiences,* and *Attitude* as ways of discovering *Meaning in Life.* This Meaning-Action Triangle is evident in Somov's integrative method of recovery, and his countless exercises in making these concepts practical and portable; "Meaning within Addiction" can be a catalyzing proponent for change. This book is an abundant gift of possibilities for both clinician and individual in recovery treatment, or the one who wants to make any personal change in their life. *Choice Awareness Training: Logotherapy & Mindfulness Training for Treatment of Addictions,* is a clinical manual stock full of easy-to-follow methodology, theoretical explanation, validation, instruction, and guided experiential exercises for clinicians; and simultaneously, a fresh and novel "how-to" resource for all those individuals who are struggling with finding "why" they cannot seem to nip this addiction for good, and make the changes they need in order to live meaningful and fulfilling lives.

Thank you Dr. Pavel Somov for inspiring genuine hope and offering a reliable pathway out of choice-less behaviors, beyond the disease model of addictions, in order to help individuals struggling to regain their lives, their personal control, and their ability to be empowered through your Choice Awareness Training. No longer a quest with an unknown outcome, in this book we find the *Route to Recovery* and lasting change—the freedom that lies within all of us.

Marie S. Dezelic, PhD

Diplomate in Logotherapy

Author of *Meaning-Centered Therapy Workbook: Based on Viktor Frankl's Logotherapy & Existential Analysis,* and *Meaning-Centered Therapy Manual: Logotherapy & Existential Analysis Brief Therapy Protocol for Group & Individual Sessions*

www.DrMarieDezelic.com

Chapter 1
From Psychology of Disease to Psychology of Choice

Compulsive behavior is, by definition, experienced as being un-free: a substance user feels compelled or driven to use. Compulsion, at a certain level of analysis, is experienced as a state of being enslaved in a pattern of repetitive behavior. This forced, driven, un-free nature of the compulsive experience is reflected both in the etymology of the cattle-prodding verb "to compel" (from the Latin compellere "to drive together," from com- "together" + pellere "to drive") and in the experiential accounts of loss of control with its corresponding DSM-IV diagnostic criterion of "unsuccessful efforts to cut down or control substance use" (APA, 1994). But who is this invisible driver that shepherds (sheep-herds) the addicted mind? What is this presumed ominous entity that takes over the steering wheel of human volition to drive us into a functional abyss as we take the backseat to our appetites and drives? Is addictive behavior really compulsive, in the sense of being driven by an external force that is outside of our control? Or is addictive behavior nothing more than a choice that has become a habit?

How one answers these questions (if such questions are even posed in the still expanding days of the Disease Model reductionism) determines the therapeutic ceiling of recovery. A person who might have previously thought that he or she chose to engage in the appetitive behavior but who has eventually come to conceptualize such behavior as being compulsive, has, in a sense, shifted away from the ontological position of free will (a responsible stance of driving) and internalized a position of existential passivity and determinism (a victimized stance of being driven). With this in mind, a key humanistic challenge of recovery from substance use and other compulsive spectrum disorders appears to be a recovery of one's sense of freedom to choose, to act freely, to determine one's behavior, and to control the controllable aspects of one's life. And, indeed, without a regained sense of freedom-to-change, how can a journey of change even begin? Change, after all, is psychologically predicated on a perceived freedom to choose a novel path, an alternative course of action, a different way. Recovery from compulsive behavior without the recovery of one's sense of control and agency is behavioral rehabilitation without existential rehabilitation. The proponents of the Disease Model of addiction (that, on inspection, is nothing more than a reified metaphor) are at least consistent: when viewed through the deterministic lens of incurable disease, one can never be recovered. Indeed, if we diagnostically define addiction as being accompanied by a sense of loss of control, treatment that only eliminates the compulsive behavior without reinstating a sense of control falls short of recovery and is nothing more than symptom management.

Disease Model of Addiction and the Decline of Will

Allen Wheelis in his 1958 book, The Quest for Identity, sounded a civilization-wide bell of alarm as he wrote about the emerging "decline of will" (p. 42). Wheelis noted that "since Renaissance, man's sense of freedom has increased to a point probably unequalled in any prior civilization, achieving such expressions as 'I am the master of my fate; I am the captain of my soul." But as the "material universe" was found to be more and more "rigorously determined," "the concept of will has passed into partial eclipse." Wheelis noted that as an ever-growing number of patients doubted "the efficacy of will," so did the clinicians that treated them: after all, "the same culture produces both" (pp. 43-44).

As the term "will-power" – among the clinically "sophisticated" – has become an "unambiguous badge of naiveté," one's attempts "to force one's way out of a conditioned of neurotic misery" became an unadvisable "counterphobic maneuver" (p. 44). What used to be a strength became a weakness, and viewing the controllable behavior as symptoms of an uncontrollable and incurable disease of addiction became a cure-all.

A confession of a disease of addiction as panacea? Powerlessness as power? What paradox! In what could be seen as prophetic anticipation of the reign of the Disease Model of addiction, Wheelis remarked: "in our understanding of human nature we have gained determinism and lost determination – though these two things are neither coordinate nor incompatible."

Bruce Wilshire, in his 1998 book Wild Hunger: The Primal Roots of Modern Addiction, writing forty years after Wheelis, echoes the same existential sentiment: "to regard addiction as a disease is well-intentioned, but it is a de facto insult to human beings," and adds that the "great price" of viewing addiction as "something that happens to us" is the loss of one's sense of freedom, of "the immediate sense of oneself as an ongoing source of initiatives in the world, a real power, an agent" (p. 97). What does Wilshire possibly mean by the "well-intentioned" mandate of the Disease Model? In trying to combat the moralizing of the Temperance view of substance use as sinful, the Disease Model medically mainstreamed substance use treatment and, thus, spared legions of substance users from the moral scorn of society. But in this unmistakably humanistic attempt to extricate chemical coping from the shadows of "sin," the Disease Model overshot: the "baby" of human self-determination, agency, freedom and will has been thrown out along with the "bathwater" of moralizing.

It is a philosophical banality to say that there is no freedom without responsibility. Applied to the challenge of substance use treatment, it would seem just as banal to proclaim that there can be no recovery of a sense of control as long as the prevailing treatment ideology externalizes one's free choice (to engage in a given behavior) to the specter of disease. It would seem that to view substance use as conditioned, habitual, self-medicating, self-regulatory, coping behavior is intuitive, but apparently it is not. Many have tried to ram the "well-intentioned" bastion of the Disease Model with facts and eloquent argumentation: Stanton Peele (with his 1989 Diseasing of America), Glenn Walters (with his 1999 The Addiction Concept), Jeffrey Schaler (with his 1999

Addiction is a Choice). But seemingly to no major avail. Peele, Walters and Schaler aren't some clinical Stoics peddling "can-do" spirit. These are compassionate clinicians trying to advocate for their patients' most inalienable psychological right, the right for self-determination.

So, then, what's the matter? Why haven't these books resulted in a humanizing reform of the recovery industry? The problem might have to do with the fact that the addiction-as-a-choice model is experientially counter-intuitive. "If I can quit, then why haven't I quit?" – this sentiment, unless unaddressed, is the stumbling stone of the addiction-as- a-choice model. Peele, Walters, and Schaler, if we may extrapolate from their writings, are philosophically versed thinkers who are ontologically and strategically convinced of free will. Yet the majority of the patients seeking help with problematic substance use are preoccupied with tactical goals: they are in search of immediate symptom relief and, as such, are not attuned to the fundamentally existential context of their presentations. A sense of loss of control and feeling compelled to use, i.e. feeling experientially un-free and enslaved by compulsion, is a quintessential issue of existence. To rehabilitate behavior and to fail to rehabilitate the perceived loss of control is to ignore the phenomenological heart of the matter.

This is where Logotherapy (Frankl, 1969) comes in. While Logotherapy is uniquely positioned to address the existential subtext of such substance-use related concerns as perceived loss of control (Somov, 2007), the clinical proponents of the addiction-as-a-choice model run the risk of putting their clients on the defensive when they begin with the conclusions of their philosophical musings, rather than from the beginning, with a Socratic style discussion of the underlying concepts.

The ontological journey from the perceived loss of control to re- conceptualizing addiction as habitual mindlessness and re-conceptualizing recovery as re-gaining a sense of control (as well as behavior modification) has to commence at the beginning, with the validation of the sense of loss of control. A habitual substance user does, indeed, feel that he or she has no choice but to use. This feeling of being un-free, of course, does not negate the fact that the user is technically free to act as he or she pleases. But, to resort to another philosophical banality, perception is reality; and it is the task of the clinician to assist the client to go beyond this perception of being un-free by discussing the psychology of freedom which is the psychology of choice awareness.

Psychology of Freedom, Choice and Change

Psychology of freedom, psychology of choice, and psychology of change are irrevocably intertwined since freedom manifests through awareness of a choice and since there can be no change with a choice to think or act differently. The notion of "choice" refers to: a) the awareness of there being two or more options available to choose from, and to b) the act of selection of one of the options available. The perceptual awareness of options is what gives us a sense of freedom. The behavioral act of selection of options is the process of change. Restated, choice is both an awareness of options that creates a sense of freedom, and an act of selection of the option that constitutes the fact of change. Therefore, freedom-to-choose is freedom-to-change.

Chapter 2
The Change Equation

The Change Equation, or the Motivational Enhancement, Choice Awareness, and Use Prevention Therapy (Somov & Somova, 2003), is a proposed algorithm of change intended as a theoretical platform for the treatment of the compulsive/addictive spectrum of psychological presentations. The mandate of applied psychology is that of facilitating change, from one state to another. The Change Equation proposes the following "equation" of change:

Change = Freedom to Change + Reason to Change + Method to Change

The Change Equation model begins with the thesis that a sense of freedom to change is primary: one has to recognize oneself as being free (i.e. capable) in order to endeavor a change. While reason to change (motivation for change) is important, it is at best predictive of an attempt at change. Method to change (which involves the mastery of change- specific skills such as craving control or emotional self-regulation) serves to predict the successful maintenance of change once it has been endeavored, but only if the person remains aware of the choice to utilize the skills whenever necessary.

Barriers to Agency: Automaticity and Schemas

The Change Equation model recognizes that a sense of being free to change (agency), while an ontologically inalienable constant, is a perceptual variable. And indeed, while, in theory, at any given moment, we have at least two or more options (or degrees of freedom) to choose from, we often feel that we have no choice. In other words, while the fact of our actual freedom is a constant, our perceptual freedom is a variable that is limited by cognitive-behavioral automaticity and freedom- restricting belief schemas. Cognitive-behavioral automaticity is thinking (interpretive) and acting habits, i.e. schematic

15

reactivity that is devoid of conscious awareness of response choices available at a given moment. Such automaticity results in mindlessness that "narrows our choices" (Langer, 1989, p. 55). Freedom-restricting belief structures (such as a premature cognitive commitment to the Disease Model of addiction) are maladaptive conceptualizations of the problem that restrict one's perceived capacity for change.

Total Freedom-to-Change: Strategic and Tactical Choice Awareness

Clients' sense of freedom-to-change is facilitated through Choice Awareness Training that involves cultivation of both strategic and tactical choice awareness. Cultivation of clients' strategic sense of being free is accomplished through a systematic challenging of clients' freedom-restricting belief schemas, and is designed to leverage an ontological shift to a baseline (strategic) realization that one always has a choice in any matter, that one cannot not choose, and that, as a result, one is fundamentally free, free to choose, and, thus, to change. Successfully instilled sense of freedom (to choose and, therefore, to change) has no "half-life" and offers an open-ended interpretive relapse prevention buffer against failed efforts at change.

Knowing that one is fundamentally free is only theory, however empowering it might be. In practice, an operational, tactical of being free manifests through choice awareness, i.e. through the awareness of the options that are immediately given to us. If I am aware of no options, then, phenomenologically, I have no choice, and, therefore, I am not free since there is nothing to choose from. Thus, a here-and-now awareness of options is a prerequisite for an act of choice and for a corresponding sense of being free. This tactical sense of freedom is a function of the number of consciously perceived options at any given time out of all the potential options available to an individual in any given moment. Consequently, tactical (actionable, realizable, pragmatic) freedom is directly proportionate to the degree of choice awareness: the greater the awareness of the choice options available at any given moment, the greater is the degree of freedom.

In summary, from the standpoint of the Change Equation model of change, in order for change to occur (assuming the reason to change and the method to change), one must:

a) become strategically aware of one's fundamental freedom to choose, and, thus, to change;

b) re-conceptualize the perceived loss of control as being a function of habit-associated automaticity, and

c) develop a habit of being tactically aware of the options available in any given moment, particularly at the times of making change-relevant decisions which is facilitated through an increased baseline of choice awareness with the help of daily choice awareness practice.

On a technical level, Choice Awareness Training consists of a combination of Logotherapy (to promote ontological, strategic, existential sense of always having a choice and, thus, being fundamentally free) and modified Mindfulness Training (to promote tactical, here-and-now awareness of immediately given choice options). Choice Awareness Training was piloted in the context of a correctional residential drug and alcohol treatment program in an American jail, as part of an overall clinical curriculum predicated on the Change Equation model (Somov & Somova, 2003).

Chapter 3
Freedom-to-Change: Conceptual Differentiation

Freedom-to-Change and Self-Efficacy

Bandura (1977) defined Self-Efficacy as a person's belief in (or confidence in) his or her ability to successfully carry out a specific task. Freedom-to-Change is a belief that one is fundamentally free to change, i.e. that one is free to perform or "can" perform a given task.

The "can-do-ism" of Self-Efficacy and the "can-do-ism" of Choice Awareness Training, as similar as they may seem, are fundamentally different issues. The "can-do-ism" of Self-Efficacy, with self-efficacy being defined as confidence in one's ability to succeed, is a probability of success issue, whereas the "can-do-ism" of the Freedom-to-Change is a capability issue. The Freedom-to-Change construct is designed to reflect the species-wide range of human capability (is a given endeavor within my human capacity?); whereas the construct of Self-Efficacy is a person- specific estimation of the probability-of-success (will I succeed at this endeavor if I were to attempt it?). With these distinctions in mind, the thrust of Choice Awareness Training is not to nurture the client's belief that he or she will successfully carry out a specific task, but to nurture the client's realization that he or she can carry out the task in question. With this distinction in mind, it could be said that the "can-do-ism" of Self-Efficacy is really a "will-do-ism."

This conceptual differentiation might seem like clinically insignificant hair-splitting. But it isn't: the difference between Freedom- to-Change (which delineates one's capability) and Self-Efficacy (which predicts the probability that a given action will be taken) is no less significant than the difference between capability and motivation. If treatment fails to differentiate between the constant of "capability" (can-do) and the variable of motivation-contingent "probability" (will-do), the individual, faced with a lapse or a relapse, is certain to attribute his or her failure to lacking "capability," i.e. to being globally unable and incapable to meet and maintain the recovery goals. This catastrophized "I can't do this!" conclusion will, unfortunately, take the place of an otherwise more self-accepting conclusion of "I know I can do this, but I have not yet succeeded in doing so."

From Freedom-to-Change to Readiness-to-Change

The transition through the initial stages of readiness-to-change (Prochaska & DiClemente, 1986) might be arrested by a client's sense of inefficacy. Miller and Rollnick (1991) recognized the need to enhance the client's self-efficacy (i.e. client's belief in his or her ability to successfully carry out the tasks of recovery) as part of motivational enhancement.

Given the above-delineated distinction between self-efficacy and one's sense of being fundamentally free to choose, and, thus, to change, it would appear that the ambivalence of the Precontemplation stage might be just as much about whether one can change as it is about whether one will be able to change. The "I want to, but I am not sure if I can" ambivalence appears to be phenomenologically precede the "I can, but I am not sure if I want to" ambivalence. And, indeed, in order to motivationally vacillate as to whether one wants to change or not, one would have to first presuppose that the very change in question is even possible.

Furthermore, a client who appears to be motivationally ambivalent, i.e. seemingly unsure if he or she wants to proceed with the tasks of recovery, might be merely questioning whether he or she can, in fact, change. With these considerations in mind, it is recommended here that Choice Awareness Training (as a means to developing one's sense of Freedom-to-Change) should ideally precede the cultivation of the Reasons to Change or, at the very least, proceed in parallel with motivational enhancement.

Freedom-to-Change through Lonergan's Lens

Lonergan's Operational Range of Freedom
Lonergan (Tengan, 1999) draws a distinction between Essential freedom and Effective freedom that somewhat parallels this author's distinction between Strategic and Tactical Awareness of Freedom to Change (or strategic and tactical freedom). Tengan clarifies Lonergan's dichotomy as follows: whereas "essential freedom is concerned with possible courses of action, effective freedom is concerned with the actual courses of action" with the effective freedom being, in essence, an "operational range at a person's disposal" (p. 94).
Limitations to the Operational Range of Freedom
Lonergan posits the following 4 barriers to this operational range of freedom.

1) *External Circumstance*: one's effective freedom can be restricted by an External Circumstance. For example, if you are five feet tall your chances of being drafted into NBA are inherently limited by the fact that one's height is an important prerequisite for professional-level basketball.

2) *Psychoneural State or Subject's Sensitivity*: Lonergan posits that one's "capacity for deliberation and choice" can be hampered by such neurotic phenomena as anxiety or obsessions. For example, an otherwise perfectly able youth of adequate height and basketball skill might be hesitant to pursue a career in basketball out of the perfectionistic dread of failure.

3) *Subject's Intelligence*: Lonergan explains that one's operational range of freedom is, to an extent, a matter of one's intellectual development. Consequently, one's fund of knowledge, education, analytical capacity all play a factor in one's "capacity for deliberation and choice." In other words, the more one knows and the better one processes information, the freer one is.

4) *Universal Willingness*: Lonergan recognizes habit as an impediment to an essential free choice and advocates the development of universal willingness in accordance with which a person is "antecedently willing to learn all there is to learn about willing and learning and about the enlargement of one's freedom from external circumstance and psychoneural interferences." In other words, Lonergan proposes that to expand one's effective freedom, a person has to maintain an overall appreciation of how habits create response inclinations (or response orientations that manifest as a willingness to respond in a specific manner) and to cultivate a kind of universal willingness to act freely rather than out of a habitual response inclination.

Lonergan's Universal Willingness

Lonergan's Universal Willingness, if defined as a willingness to act freely (willingly), rather than out of habitual inclinations (automatically), comes satisfyingly close to this author's conception of Strategic Awareness of the Freedom to Change. The notion of Universal Willingness, however, appears insufficient to enable an awareness of the freedom to change at any given moment in the person's life. In much the same fashion as the Strategic Awareness of the Freedom to Change, Universal Willingness exists as a dormant realization, as a stored philosophy, a guiding principle that may or may not be incorporated into one's thought content at any given time-point. And as such, for all intents and purposes, Universal Willingness or Strategic Awareness of the Freedom to Change is only useful as a philosophical and motivational impetus to developing a capacity for Tactical Awareness of the Freedom to Change.

Consequently, it could be said that Lonergan's four impediments to the effective range of freedom need to be complimented by the fifth impediment, i.e. lack of baseline (moment-by-moment) choice awareness. And, indeed, a person who is otherwise non-restricted by circumstance, who is psychoneurally regulated or stable, who is both intellectually adequate, and who, otherwise, knows and appreciates the need to be unimpaired by the response momentum of the habits, might be factually mindless, very much in the process of enacting a given habit, entirely oblivious to the options or possibilities available at any given time. What appears to be required, therefore, is not a philosophical willingness to act freely but an experiential baseline of awareness or tactical awareness of the fact that one can act freely or willingly at any given moment. As demonstrated above, both Bandura's and Lonergan's conceptual equivalents of a sense of freedom-to-change (self-efficacy and universal willingness, respectively) suffer from one and the same fundamental problem of application. While both are essentially conceptual reformulations of one's capacity for freedom and self-control, neither approach provides a method for developing an experiential baseline of awareness or tactical awareness of one's freedom to change.

Glasser's Responsibility Training versus Choice Awareness Training

William Glasser, M.D., the founder of Reality Therapy, was one of the few 20th century North American psychotherapy designers who appeared to appreciate, at least implicitly, the need for choice awareness training. Responsibility, the second of Glasser's "3 Rs" is defined as "ability to fulfill one's needs, and to do so in a way that *does not deprive others of their ability to fulfill their needs*" (Glasser, 1965). Glasser further notes in the same text that "teaching of responsibility is the most important task of all higher animals, man most certainly included."

Glasser's Moralism versus Humanism of Choice Awareness

Glasser's italics ("a way that does not deprive others of their ability to fulfill their needs") and the third of his "3 Rs," Right-and-Wrong, show an alliterative hint of the faintly mo-RRR-alistic g-RRR-owl of his clinical orientation, which, in my opinion, served to be the unfortunate demise of an otherwise perfectly sound idea of choice awareness training. Glasser, in my opinion, in focusing on the Responsibility side of the coin of Freedom, got it backwards. He was basing his therapeutic sales pitch on the Cost, rather than the Benefit, on Responsibility rather than Freedom, on Consequence rather than Choice. With that in mind, his otherwise empowering and humanistic affirmation of "one's ability to fulfill one's needs" (choice, freedom) was drowned in the moralistic emphasis on responsibility. It is of note that in its dismissal of the concept of mental illness, and holding clients responsible for their symptoms, Glasser's take does parallel this author's dismissal of the notion of addiction as a disease. Similar to Glasser, the position offered in this approach prompts a substance user to take responsibility for their using behavior by highlighting the fundamental capacity for choice that one possesses at any given time, if he or she is sufficiently choice-aware or awake.

Unlike the undisguised moralism of Glasser's Reality Therapy, the Change Equation approach humanistically normalizes our predisposition for automaticity and mindlessness, with a resultant sense of being out of control and without a choice, and encourages the individual to regain self- control without the suggestion of any particular value-based treatment goals.

Choice Awareness Training vs. Willpower

The act of will, application of willpower, and making of a choice are synonymous. The term willpower, however, has an unfortunate connotation of varying strength, as if to convey that some people have a more powerful will than others. It should be noted that the term "willpower" is not an inherently incorrect term. When used in the sense of "power of will (or volition)," the term heightens, if not extols, the human capacity to make a choice. The phrase "power of will" is free from any kind of interpersonal comparison, it is merely an acknowledgement that as humans we possess a power (a freedom) of self-determination through choice. The term "willpower" becomes problematic, however, when the semantic focus shifts from "power of will" to "how powerful one's will is." The Concise American Heritage Dictionary (1987) reflects this distinction by defining "will power" as a) the ability to carry out one's decisions, wishes, or plans, and b) the strength of mind. While the first meaning of willpower does exist, the second is nothing but a linguistic connotation of the word "power" that does not have a phenomenological reality. Comparative perception of will or capacity for choice as being stronger or weaker is erroneous and psychologically damaging. An act of will or a choice is a binary event: one either acts or does not act in a certain fashion. Consequently, all people are equally strong choosers, with an equal power for will, i.e. of the same willpower. While equal in willpower, i.e. in the capacity for choice, people differ in:

a) how they apply their will/choice, and in
b) the degree of their conscious awareness of their capacity for choice.

Pertaining to a), it is easy to see how judging of others' actions leads to a conclusion that so and so has weak will. It is the belief of this author that the process of moral comparison is the historical context for the emergence of the term willpower. Say a person is faced with an opportunity to steal something of value. He/she is tempted and, then, he acts upon that temptation. To an outsider, this might seem like a battle between wanting to steal and not wanting to steal that has been resolved in the favor of the presumed temptation: the person could not withstand the promise of easy money, the allure of a financial short-cut. Implicit in such interpretation is that one is weak since he surrendered, gave in to the temptation. A verdict of weak willpower or not having enough willpower is the next logical step in such a chain of interpretation.

An alternative view of the situation is that one did not surrender or give in to the temptation. One merely chose to act upon his desire to steal – for a variety of personal reasons. According to such interpretation there is no weakness of will, there is only socially unacceptable misapplication of one's will. Consequently, the notion of strong or weak power appears to be a result of moralistic judgment in which there is an automatic semi- religious implication that when faced with socially unsanctioned opportunities (drugs, sex, crime) people are taunted, tempted, lured by whatever is the cultural equivalent of the devil or the dark side and the weakest give in. With this in mind, the notion of willpower has become a kind of implicit morality yard-stick that in the context of substance use treatment represents a circular double-bind, a kind of logical dead-end, a questionable asset in the change process. In reality, people merely make choices that we may or may not agree with – and our disagreement has nothing to do with the measurement of a given person's capacity for choice. Just because one person insightfully chooses to "numb out" in order not to "go ballistic," it does not mean that he or she has weak will – all it means is that at this moment this person had concluded (rightly or incorrectly) that drinking or drugging was a strategy of choice, a calculated act of emotional self-regulation.

Pertaining to b) (above), mindless, reflexive, knee-jerk decisions seem "weak" since they are void of the power of conscious choosing. Such unconscious decisions seem "weak" because in their unconsciousness they fail to represent the best interests of the chooser. This is exactly the case when a person in recovery yields to a craving, to an impulse to use. To an outsider, such an easy surrender to a craving appears like an act of weak will. In reality, the weakness of the act stems from its conditioned unconsciousness (or habitual automaticity) rather than from the actor's actual capacity to resist a craving impulse. An unconscious choice is like a sleeping beauty whose charms are not in play while she is dormant. The "Gun Point Test" is evidence enough that any seemingly weak-willed person would be capable of resisting a craving, given an opportunity to do so in a fully "awakened" state.

The therapeutic importance of deconstructing the myth of willpower cannot be overemphasized. When one buys into the notion of willpower and uses lack of it as an excuse to use, he or she is beyond criticism. In such a case, willpower adopts the rationalizing benefit of the doubt that ensures the belief in addiction as a medical disease. To ask a weak person to do something they do not have the strength for is akin to Baron Munchausen's pulling himself out of the swamp by his own pony-tail. In other words, change based on willpower is similar to asking one to be strong when one is weak.

People in recovery who have uncritically bought into the notion of will- power are well familiar with this double bind: they are asked to use willpower to stay away from drugs and alcohol, to stay in control; but if they had the willpower to stay away from the drugs and alcohol in the first place they probably would have not been out of control to begin with. With these considerations in mind, it is important to dissect the myth of willpower as a volitional muscle that varies in size from one person to another, and to substitute this hazardous term with a notion that everyone has the exact same capacity for choice. Therefore, when one says "I can't" they are really saying "I won't."

It should be pointed out that traditional substance use treatment models make the error of omission in not directly debunking the myth of will- power. Contrary to this, the present approach incorporates the discussion of the interplay between the notions of will-power and choice into the session curriculum.

Comment on the Strength of Willpower Research Baumeister et al. (1994) present the findings of research (Wegner et al. (1990), Pennebaker & Chew (1985), Notarius et al (1982), Waide and Orne (1982)) that suggests that self-regulation, empirically defined as self-stopping, involves not only mental but physical exertion as well as evidenced by increased psychophysiological arousal. In interpreting the results of various research teams, Baumeister et al (1994) conclude that chronically weak willpower may be one of the three possible impediments to self-regulation. In particular, they write that "it is almost certainly true that some people have more self-discipline than others, are better able to control their actions and feelings, are more capable of resisting temptation" (p. 19). They further proceed to metaphorically liken self- regulatory capacity (and, by implication, willpower) to a muscle whose strength can be both weakened and strengthened over time by precedents of self-regulation or failures thereof. While the research on the physical exertion aspect of self-stopping/self-regulatory processes appears to be beyond methodological doubt, Baumeister's conclusion that some people are "better able to control their actions and feelings" and are "more capable of resisting temptation" (Baumeister et al., 1994, p. 19) appears to be an unwarranted leap of logic. The self-stopping research cited by Baumeister et al. made no inter-group comparisons.

Consequently, while Baumeister et al. speculate that differences in will- power would account for the presumed differences in degree of control over actions and feelings, and resistance to temptations, this author believes that whatever interpersonal differences exist in terms of these parameters, they are strictly a function of differences in motivation and skill-power, not in will-power. In equating "capacity for self-regulation" with will-power, Baumeister et al. (1994, p. 19) appear to mistake a decision to self-regulate with the effectiveness of the execution of such a decision which is predicated on the motivation to self-regulate, self- regulation skill-level, and, at risk of being methodologically pedantic, on such additional impediments to effective freedom as psychoneuronal state and subject's intellectual development (Lonergan).

With this in mind, to justify the conclusion by Baumeister et al. that some people have more will-power than others (not just better self-regulation skill than others), there would need to be a study protocol that finds interpersonal differences in self-stopping after partialing out or controlling for any differences in

27

motivation to self-regulate, self-regulatory skill- level, intellectual development, and subjects' psychoneuronal reactivity. To this author's knowledge, no such research has been published to date.

Overview: Goals of Choice Awareness Training

Choice Awareness Training pursues the following three goals:

1) *Development of a Strategic Awareness of Freedom to Change* as evidenced by an appreciation of choice as a manifestation of fundamental, inevitable freedom that potentiates the change process.

Clients are expected to internalize the fact that they "cannot not choose," that at any given time they have a choice and, consequently, hold the freedom to act as they choose, in accordance with their goals, and the responsibility for any subsequent benefits and costs of their choice.

2) *Reformulation of the Perceived Chronicity of Addiction and Loss of Control* as being a function of normal human functioning/habit formation/coping automatization.

Clients discard such self-deprecatory conceptions about their prior inability to change as "lacking will-power" or "being hooked," and are helped to understand that while they "cannot not choose," their freedom to change or to make choices can be limited by perfectly human proneness to mindless, stimulus-response bound, conditioned, auto-piloted and schematic functioning. Clients further appreciate that they can both proactively prevent and retroactively terminate auto-piloted, schematic functioning through the practice of choice awareness (overall message of this section is that "you cannot not choose unless you are on a mindless, thoughtless, conditioned, self-unaware autopilot")

3) *Development of a Tactical Awareness of Freedom to Change* through: a) the facilitated, in-session, behaviorally-experiential practice of choice awareness, and b) a formulation of and implementation of a choice- awareness regimen (the overall message of this section is that the "daily choice awareness practice is key to executing a target change").

Choice Awareness Training and Controlled Use
Choice Awareness Training can help save the lives of those who have an unshakable commitment to alcohol and/or drug use, be it for the reasons of their particular world-view, or anti-social personality orientation, or, more commonly, because of convincing personal data that evidenced their capacity for controlled use. Let's face it: the current establishment of the substance use treatment industry in the United States (with the exception of such isolated controlled use advocates as Marlatt) has little, if anything, to offer to a substance user, who, even after a non-judgmental motivational enhancement, decides in favor of using. When it comes down to a client with a controlled use agenda, it should be appreciated that Choice Awareness training is a control-training system, and as such Choice Awareness Training can help translate the client's intention for controlled use into a more attainable reality.

Arguments of Spiritual Determinism in the Context of Choice Awareness Training

The content of Choice Awareness Training is non-faith-based. Any religious or fatalistic remarks about pre-determined destiny, fate, or God's will are to be respectfully re-directed. When such comments cannot be disregarded and require attention, clinicians are encouraged not to disagree but to reframe the notion of choice at a micro (moment-by-moment, day- to-day) level, not at a macro (cosmic/spiritual) level.

Chapter 4

Part I of Choice Awareness Training:
Cultivating Strategic Freedom to Change

This part of Choice Awareness Training can be conceptualized as a curriculum of themes, the discussion of which helps clients cultivate a strategic, philosophical, ontological awareness of their freedom as a fundamental human condition. This takes the form of a part-didactic, part-Socratic dialogue with the client about their capacity for choice, and, thus, change. The following are themes and exercises that constitute this part of Choice Awareness Training.

Reframing the Addiction as a Habit, not a Disease

Facilitators take clients on a conceptual head-on collision with the Disease Model of addiction. Addiction is reframed in the context of operant conditioning theory and the Disease Model of Addiction is challenged. This is accomplished through the review of the history of the Disease Model of addiction (for excellent coverage of these topics, please, refer to Peele's "Diseasing of America," Schaler's "Addiction is a Choice," and Walters' "The Concept of Addiction"). The logical inconsistencies of the concept of addiction as a disease and of the 12 Steps are reviewed.

In particular, facilitators should be prepared to recognize the following errors in logic. Petitio principii is the logical fallacy of tautology in which the same premise serves as both the premise and the conclusion (Walters, 1999). Facilitators need to familiarize themselves with the tautology of the loss of control argument (in which the loss of control serves both to describe and explain addiction), the prediction tautology (a problem drinker can never drink in moderation and any drinker that can drink in moderation is not a problem drinker), and the denial tautology (any disagreement with the Disease

Model of addiction constitutes proof of disease) (Walters, 1999).

Review of Self-Change Literature

Clients are introduced to self-change literature, the study of the phenomenon of self-change among drug and alcohol users, an emerging empirical body of research that contradicts the postulates of the Disease Model of addiction. The self-change literatures helps address the logical fallacy of the *argumentum ad verecundian* (an argument that involves an appeal to authority to establish credibility, in the case of the Disease Model of addiction, this argument involves an appeal to medical authority, whereas in the case of the 12 Step paradigm, the argument involves the appeal to the spiritual authority of the "higher power") (Walters, 1999). Studies show that self-change "appears to be the dominant pathway to recovery" (Klingemann et al, 2001, p. 21). Facilitators present self-change statistics with a particular emphasis on the longitudinal stability of natural recovery.

Langer, in her 1989 book, entitled "Mindfulness," shares the results of a study that supports the importance of exposing individuals in recovery to various conceptualizations of recovery. In particular, Langer shares that in a study of forty-two patients attending an alcohol clinic, the individuals "who had been exposed to only one model of alcoholism" (early in their lives) "appeared to have developed mindsets so rigid that the options offered by therapy did not seem available to them," whereas "those who had been successfully helped in therapy virtually always came from the multiple role-model group" (1989, p. 52). Langer suggests that subscribing to a genetic/medical view of addiction constitutes a counter- therapeutic "premature cognitive commitment" to a particular model of recovery, and notes that "alcoholics who see the cause of their problem as purely genetic seem to give up the control that could help their recovery" (p. 51). Helping clients review the findings of self-change literature introduces alternative views on recovery and safeguards against an unnecessarily fore-shortened clinical diagnosis.

Review of Client's Personal Self-Change/Success Data & Challenging of All-or-Nothing View of Self-Control

Furthermore, clients who express skepticism about the validity of self- change literature are encouraged to explore their own self-change data. The clients' belief in their powerlessness over addiction is likely to be a function of a) an uncritically adopted belief that they are powerless, a kind of iatrogenic ideological side-effects of past treatments that were informed by the Disease Model of addiction, and b) dichotomous/perfectionistic/all- or-nothing thinking that led clients to dismiss the partial success of their past self-change efforts.

With this in mind, the Review of Personal Self-Change Data allows the client to learn from his successes rather than to continue to focus on his failures with an inevitable sense of loss of control. More specifically, clients are encouraged to think of at least one precedent of controlling their desire to use. It is simply inconceivable that a substance user had never to postpone his using, that he or she always used whenever he or she desired to use.

The facilitator explores clients' abstinence histories, times when they had to wait until the next day to use because they had to "pee in the cup," and they could not afford another dirty urine out of fear of losing employment or violating the conditions of their parole. Facilitators may focus on the times when the clients wanted to use but had no financial means to cop the drug and, therefore, had to figure out ways to get money be it by stealing, or taking the TV or their car stereo to the pawn shop, or by doing some work to get the money. The review and verbalization of these use-postponement precedents is significant in that each such episode demonstrates to the client that – regardless of the intensity of their urges – they had been able to control their behavior for varying periods of time on numerous occasions. The conclusion – as logically inevitable as it may seem – is likely to require additional processing. The client should be assisted to appreciate the meaning of these brief and not-so-brief periods of abstinence: they have, in fact, exercised control over their using behavior. If they can control an urge for a brief duration of time, they can control it for any duration of time, given the proper motivational incentive, and, particularly, when augmented with more than intuitive skill-power and self-regulation tools.

In review, the idea behind this particular strategy is to de-dichotomize the all-or-nothing cognitive distortion: just because the clients could not control their using behavior all of the time, it does not mean that is not controllable, as evidenced by the numerous times in the life of any substance user when he or she does, in fact, succeed in controlling their using behavior for some duration of time. The consistent objection that is voiced at this point is a sudden re-interpretation of the problem: whereas in the past the problem was conceptualized behaviorally (drinking or drugging, using behavior), now it is re-interpreted cognitively as a problem of the constant craving. In particular, the clients concede that, yes, they now realize that, assuming adequate motivation, they can control their behavior, what they cannot control, however, is the desire to use. This objection, if voiced, is the opportunity to normalize and de- pathologize the fact of the craving. Drug and/or alcohol craving can be re- interpreted as a perfectly legitimate desire for relief of stress, for a sense of well-being, that can be fulfilled in psychologically-, legally-, physically-, and financially-safer ways. Craving for a relief or well-being is, therefore, portrayed as a normal vital sign, a human response to the intermittent reality of pain and suffering.

Discussing the Implications of the Disease-Model Explanatory Style

Individuals with a pessimistic explanatory style develop a sense of helplessness and give up in the face of failure or extreme challenge (Satterfield, 2000). The disease concept of addiction is a paragon of the pessimistic explanatory style. The attribution theory research defines pessimistic explanatory style as a causal model that attributes the causes of a negative event to internal, stable, and global factors (Abramson, Seligman, & Teasdale, 1978). The disease model of addiction encapsulates all three. A sense of powerlessness, therefore, is a logical by-product of the pessimistic explanation of addiction as a disease and constitutes learned helplessness. Choice Awareness Training, in a manner consistent with positive psychology, helps clients appreciate that learned helplessness is not factual helplessness, and helps clarify the distinction between feeling helpless and being helpless.

Tackling the Issue of the Pre-Disposition

The notion of a pre-disposition is often misunderstood by clients. Pre- dispositions pre-determine certain needs, not the specific means with which these needs are met. If a person is predisposed for anxiety spectrum disorders, he or she has at least four options to self-regulate:

> 1) psychological self-help,
> 2) psychopharmacology, and
> 3) chemical self- help through substance use (as a form of self-psychiatry).

Facilitators work to counter the fatalistic understanding of the notion of pre-disposition, reinforced by the fear-mongering Disease Model of addiction, and help clients realize that whatever pre-dispositions they might have, they are still fundamentally free to choose a particular method for addressing any biological, genetic, or chemical deficits that they might have.

Taking on the Issue of Addictive Personality

The notion of Addictive Personality failed to acquire empirical support in over half a century of scientific investigation (Miller and Rollnick, 1991). Clients are helped to see that the pathologizing connotation of "addictive personality" is merely a function of social stigma attached to a given appetite. Furthermore, with the word "addiction" seen in the context of operant conditioning, the very construct of "addictive personality" can be reframed as "habit-forming personality," which, of course, is universally possessed.

Discussing Habit Formation

If "addiction" is to be effectively re-conceptualized as a habit, not a disease, discussion of the process of habit formation is of paramount importance. Discussion of habit formation (of habit psychology) offers a normalizing, validating, explanation of how over-learned habits can lead to a sense of loss of control, without the counter-therapeutic externalizing that stems from the notion that has no control because of a presumed disease of addiction.

Habits have been often referred to as "second nature." The notion of "second nature" is a semantic gold mine that holds a phenomenological clue to the mystery of the sense of loss of control. Tengan (1999), in clarifying Lonergan's teachings on habit formation, notes that "a habit gives an inclination to an otherwise indeterminate potency (the will)," and, as a result, "predetermining us to act in certain directions" (p.97). Consequently, what was once a novel, mindful, idiosyncratic response pattern becomes an over-learned natural default.

In its defaulted-ness, the acquired response pattern becomes automatic, it serves as an energy conserving short-cut. Barrett, as far back as 1911, likened the "automatism" of habits to a state "arrived at by the will when it functions evenly, simply, and regularly in a manner more or less independent of conscious attention" (1911, p. 105-141). Llinas (2001), "a founding father of the modern brain science," writing ninety years later, used, instead, the term Fixed Action Patterns to describe modules of activity "that liberate the self from unnecessarily spending time and attention on every aspect of motor and non-motor activities" (p. 134). Llinas states clearly that the rationale behind Fixed Action Patterns is "the economizing of choices" (p. 144). Whether we refer to the habits as autopilots, or schematic behavior, or second nature, or learned behavior, or fixed action patterns, this automatization "liberates" us from having to make an infinite number of minute choices. As any default, this automatization spares the mind the work of any unnecessary deliberation or decision-making, thus creating the phenomenological sense of loss of control. In a sense, a "second nature" response pattern is experienced as "happening" to the person rather than "being executed" by the person. This kind of resource-saving automatization is a hallmark achievement of the human mind. Auto-piloting or automating of various cognitive- behavioral-affective routines enables human mind to multitask as it plows through the never-ending environmental bombardment of stimuli. The loss of the sense of control (or of the sense of agency) is the cost of this optimization.

As a side note, clients are offered to examine how their uncritical acceptance of the Disease Model of addiction, in a way, represents an attempt to economize. After all, the concept of a disease ("I am doing this because I am sick) is a simple emotional conceptualization to be contrasted with a cognitively harder concept of a habit ("I am doing this because I have been conditioned to do this").

Clients are helped to appreciate the fact that the momentum of the habit, its baseline behavioral orientation, its default inclination, its automaticity with its accompanying sense of "loss of control," does not, in and of itself, negate the underlying fundamental freedom to choose same or alternative course of action. As noted above, just because an action feels "out of control," it does not mean that it is, in fact, beyond control. Lonergan described this momentum or force of the habit as the "antecedent willingness" or "unwillingness" to act in a particular manner. The "antecedent" qualifier in Lonergan's explanation is synonymous with an inclination or a default orientation towards a specific response, given a particular stimulus. The "antecedent willingness" is that phenomenological pull or drive or action-urge that predetermines a response. It should be noted and reiterated, however, that pre- determination does not equal determination. Tengan's (1999) use of the term of "voluntary habits" therefore can be understood as meaning that while, in retrospect, the execution of a habitual response might be remembered as an involuntary action, no habit is truly involuntary since any habit can be voluntarily overridden by an act of free volition (p. 96).

Consequently, any habit can be likened to pseudo-involuntarism or pseudo-choicelessness, to coin a couple of terms. Explicit discussion of how habits are experienced as involuntary defaults while being entirely within the potential control of the individual is likely to produce a self- accepting sigh of relief when clients realize that they never lost the control but that they merely neglected it.

Discussing the Power of Context (Placebo Effect)

Clients, indoctrinated by the Disease Model of addiction, may be both curious and stunned to know that the degree of intoxication is contingent on drinker's expectations and can be manipulated by modifying drinker's/user's expectations (Langer, 1989). On the basis of a review of many investigations, Langer notes that "thoughts may be a more potent determinant of the physiological reactions believed to be alcohol-related than the actual chemical properties of alcohol" (p. 183), and, in summarizing the findings of Shepard Siegel, Langer notes that "the failure of tolerance on the day of the overdose is a function of context," noting that overdoses are more likely in the unfamiliar environments.

Langer summarizes: if context has the power to change both the degree of intoxication, the severity of withdrawal symptoms, and even the effect a drug overdose, then "addiction may be more controllable than is commonly believed" (1989, p. 184). Presenting clients with the discussion of the power of situational factors offers clients much food for thought as they begin to rethink the presumed medical determinism of their addiction.

Psychoneuroimmunology as Evidence of Mind's Power over the Disease of Body

Another obvious data source to be angled against the sense of powerlessness that is secondary to uncritical acceptance of the disease model of addiction is literature on the mind-body connection. The very thrust of medicalizing addiction is to call a behavioral problem a body problem. Yet even a body problem is not immune to the solutions of the mind.

A brief sampling of psychoneuroimmunology findings can go far in helping clients who cling to the disease model to enhance a sense of control and freedom-to-change. The evidence that mind can and does solve the problems of the body is abundant enough to roll with the resistance by granting the disease model of addiction a status of "fact," while still having irrefutable and choice-enhancing arguments to augment the client's sense of efficacy. The following is a sample of the sort of facts that may help convince a disease-indoctrinated substance user of the "curability" of the incurable.
Paul Pearsall, Ph.D., in his 1987 book Superimmunity, describes the textbook example of a serious skin condition, congenital ichthyosiform erythrodemia, which is characterized by a hardening and blackening of the skin, being successfully resolved within 5 days of hypnosis by Dr. Mason. Pearsall writes that "all major dermatology textbooks report no known cure for this terrible disease" (p. 9). Yet, the fact remained that a bona fide medical problem that had been previously considered incurable was, in fact, curable through a psychological pathway. Dr. Mason's results were subsequently documented in the British Medical Journal.

Pearsall, a non-physician, reports a mind-body "miracle" in the course of which "a positive Montoux reaction (a reddening and swelling of the skin at the site of the injection of a small amount of tuberculin) was produced through injection of water by suggesting that the water injection was really tuberculin" (p. 10). Ivan Roitt, professor and head of departments of immunology and rheumatology research at the University College and Middlesex School of Medicine, in his 1991 book Essential Immunology, confirms this "popular observation concerning modulation of the delayed-type hypersensitivity Mantoux reaction in skin by hypnosis" (p. 169).

Pearsall reports other research in which a "woman experiencing a severe hay fever reaction to pollen for 12 years was helped to imagine herself free of symptoms. She became completely free of her symptoms for the first time" (p. 10). Imagine what your substance use client can do with his habit-disease if he or she cannot only imagine but evidence his freedom!

T   he sample of mind-body connection "miracles" above is but an extremely cursory fact-mining. I dove into one book and yanked out several facts that question the depressogenic notion of substance use incurability. If patients with cancer cannot only go into remission but be, in fact, pronounced "cured," why can't patients with habit problems? Facilitators that plan to use mind-body connection as an argument against the presumed incurability of the psychological (habit) problem of substance use are encouraged to bring a handful of books or articles from the field of psychoneuroimmunology or psychoimmunology and let clients browse, if they wish.

Choice Moratorium Exercise

Facilitators are encouraged to inter-lace the "fiber" of philosophizing with the "desert" of exercises. One such exercise to offer is the Choice Moratorium. The Choice Moratorimu exercises highlights the inevitability of choice. Clients are challenged to not make any choices for a pre-specified period of time (e.g. one minute). The exercise is followed with processing of the clients' reactions and insights. For additional instructions for this exercise, please, refer to Somov & Somova (2003).

The "Gun-Point Test" Hypothetical

The "Gun-Point Test" hypothetical compliments the discussion of the claim that a client has no control over drinking or drugging. In this hypothetical, clients are asked to imagine a situation in which they have an intense craving and immediate access to the substance in question. For many users, not yet convinced of the power of choice and of their potential skill-power (of craving control), this moment is well past any feasible self-regulatory "u-turn." If they are this far into it, with the drug in their hand, many will tell you that they are well on the way to use. To complete the hypothetical, add the following twist: allow the clients to imagine that someone put a gun to their head and stated: "You use – you die."

Ask the clients: "Would you use at this point?" Most clients, whether they will verbalize it or not, will admit to themselves that at a gun-point they would lay down the drug and walk away, not using it.

Ask the clients: "What does that mean?" Prepare to face the inevitable counter-argument that "Yes, but... in real life no one is going to hold a gun to your head and tell you that if you use, you die." Counter- argue along the following lines: "The gun – an inanimate object – did not introduce the choice not to use to your life, the choice was there all along, it's just that the presence of the gun helped you become aware of the choice."

The "Million Dollar Test" Hypothetical

The "Million Dollar Test" hypothetical is a variation on the theme of the "Gun Point Test." It can be used in much the same fashion to demonstrate the inevitability of choice. As would be expected, in this vignette, the clients are asked to imagine being at a point of using and having an intense desire to use. At this point, someone makes an offer they can hardly refuse: "you use – you get nothing;

you put down the drug and walk away – you get a million bucks."

A predictable but easy-to-counterargue argument is that "in real life, no one's going to give you a million bucks for not using." Counter-argue by asking the client what their recovery and freedom is worth. In this sense, any time the client passes on a drug offer he/she is enriched by priceless freedom, self-control, and clean and sober life on his/her terms. Just like in the case of the Gun-Point metaphor, the Million-Dollar metaphor demonstrates that the choice not to use was there all along, but eclipsed by the motivation to use, until the choice to use was re-eclipsed by the incentive of wealth. The incentive of wealth did not create a choice not to use, it simply brought the choice into focus.

The two metaphors described above are designed to address a substance user's paralysis of self-efficacy when in the presence of the drug or drug- related paraphernalia. While this paralysis of self-efficacy is technically a mirage of perception, it does have a phenomenological reality. This reality is predicated on numerous precedents of trying to resist the urge to use but surrendering to it when in the proximity of the drug. At this point, the clients have not yet reformulated their self-inefficacy or sense of loss of control as a function of conditioned, choice-unaware, mindless responding, and, in the absence of a better explanation, have primitively attributed the power to the drug. The following discussion helps clarify the power hierarchy between animate (human) and inanimate nature.

Demystifying the Inanimate

Substance use clinicians often hear clients verbalize the aforementioned fatalistic attitude that "once I've got my hands on it ("it" here being the drug or the paraphernalia), I can't stop." This fetishist reverence for the object is likely a reflection of the stimulus value of the paraphernalia objects with their over-conditioned "pull" to use. As part of trying to "demystify the inanimate," to highlight the passivity of the inanimate matter and its inherent dependence on the human agency, the facilitator might drop a pen down on the floor and compare the pen to an object of paraphernalia.

If the clients had been already offered Exposure & Response Prevention type craving control craving, the facilitator may more accurately simulate the moment by, say, opening a packet with sweetener and line it up on the table. The facilitator then discusses the intuitive physical reality of the fact that the simulated crack stem on the floor or the simulated line of cocaine or heroin on the table, in and of itself, cannot move or do anything on their own, let alone, control a human being. This seemingly banal discussion resets the chain of command: we, the humans, have power over the inanimate drugs and drug-related paraphernalia, not the other way around. It is the very breath that differentiates a human from a line of cocaine that is required for the inanimate substance of cocaine to become a substance use problem of a given human. This discussion often results in such revelations as "I gave it (the drug or paraphernalia) too much power, power that it doesn't really have over me." As obvious as this may sound to a non-using adult, the value of this kind of experiential "clarification" cannot be over-emphasized.

Addressing the Language Trap: "I Can't" versus "I Won't"

In the first part of the Choice Awareness Training, explicit attention should be given to how substance use clients restrict their freedom-to- change with the wall of words. Language structures perception and perception, for all intents and purposes, is reality. The facilitators' task is to help clients appreciate the interplay of language and a sense of freedom- to-change. Case in point: individuals who have internalized the 12 Step dictum of powerlessness and bought into the Disease Model of addiction are prone to confuse the "I can't" with the "I won't."

As part of Choice Awareness Training, clients are encouraged to become aware of the distinction. The "I can't" statement negates the availability of a given option. "I won't" is a matter of motivation. Whereas the "I can't" is an acknowledgement of not having a choice to perform a given act, the "I won't" is an act of choosing not to perform a given act.

For example, after instruction in and practice of craving control, clients will be assisted with understanding that while there is not a craving they "cannot" control, there might be a craving they "will not" control. While the former is an issue of choice awareness or skill-power, the latter is a function of motivation. Consequently, the fundamental distinction between the "I can't" or "I won't" is the difference in freedom-to-change and reason-to-change: while one might be free to change from one state to another at any given moment, one might not choose to change because one might not be motivated to do so. Confusing the "I won't" with the "I can't" is a process of self-deflation: each pseudo-"can't" diffuses one's sense of freedom and agency.

Language Trap (Continued): The Passive Grammar of Irresponsibility

"I am addicted," is a form of constructivist self-incarceration. This statement represents passive case grammar that, by definition, robs the person of a sense of agency. To persons that embrace this view of their substance use the world is experienced as chaotic, hard to control, unpredictable; things happen rather than get done.

In helping clients appreciate the choice-defeatist meaning of the phrase "I am addicted," I have often made synonymous parallels with the phrase "I am hooked." Being hooked means just that: being on a hook. Like a fish lured by the glistening promise of a fake bait (the drug), the user convinces himself that he is on the hook of a fishing rod of addiction. Yes, he can rigorously wiggle his tail and talk about "being sick and tired of being sick and tired," but he can't get off the hook, not himself, not without the merciful hand of a treatment provider or higher power. That is the perceptual lot of someone who believes they are hooked. But, I'd ask the client, who is holding the fishing rod of addiction? Who is the owner of the hook? Who is reeling in the client across the turbulent and murky waters to the shore of oblivion? The Inanimate Drug? The Indifferent Drug Dealer? Hardly: the owner of the hook is the client's own mind that has conceived of a notion of being without power to change.

Just like in the work of cognitive modification clients are to learn that no one can make them feel anything and therefore the passive grammar of "he made me mad" or "he made me sad" is continuously challenged, so does the passive grammar of substance user's statement that he or she is "addicted" need to be challenged and processed for its phenomenological implications.

Language Trap (Continued): The Word "Addict" and Addict Identity

Self-identification as an "addict" or an "alcoholic" is an unfortunate legacy of the 12 Step movement. While it is true that some clients use the term "addict" or "alcoholic" as a verbal short-cut to rapport building (as in "I've been through similar things, you don't have to fear my judgment, I understand where you are coming from"), the majority of self-identified "addicts" or "alcoholics" feel a kind of disempowering chronicity of their condition that does more harm than good.

A 12 Step proponent will rush to object that self-identification as "addict" or "alcoholic" is primarily designed to heighten the client's hypervigilance, to caution him or her to be on guard and watchful for any signs of lapse. While partially reasonable, this type of vigilance boomerangs. Clients come to distrust their thinking "because their best thinking got them here," and come to fear their unconscious with its treacherous and sneaky "reservations." The result is a kind of Stalinist self-regime where one's self becomes the "enemy of the people."

It goes without saying that the "addict identity" stems from buying another dangerous combination of words, namely from the notion of "addiction as a disease." Clients should be assisted with realizing that the "disease model of addiction" is a linguistic metaphor, and not the only one at that. Other metaphors are possible. For example, addiction could be metaphorically conceptualized not as a chronic disease but as an allergy. Alternatively, and in the spirit of the Change Equation, addiction can be conceptualized as a chemical self-regulation autopilot, a kind of mindless execution of a less than optimal coping strategy. With this in mind, the client should be assisted with a choice of the metaphor for their problem, with each metaphor being evaluated for its pro-change and anti-change qualities.

Such discussions often result in a realization that choosing "addict identity" (with the exception of rapport-building aspect) represents a wholesale surrender of choice. Facilitators of Change Equation approach shall respect that constructivist choice, as long as it is consciously thought out, and point out that choosing not to choose is a choice as well, and congratulate the clients on yet another consciously made choice. What shall clients call themselves instead of "addicts" or "alcoholics?" In my opinion, their actual names or the pronoun "I" would suffice. If clients do wish to categorize themselves in relation to substance use, the term "chemical coper" or "ex-chemical coper" provides conceptual continuity with the Change Equation philosophy. By calling oneself a chemical coper, the person acknowledges the fact that substance use served the purpose of emotional self-regulation. To call oneself an "ex-chemical coper" or "former chemical coper" allows the person to reiterate that they have now opted for a different coping pathway.

Discussing the Difference Between Difficult and Impossible

In facilitating client's understanding of the sense of loss of control, it is helpful to explicitly address the incremental progression of the sense of the control as the person attempts a self-stopping behavior after initiating a habitual response sequence. Zeigarnik (1938) demonstrated that a response sequence is harder to abort at the later sequence points of a given response than at the earlier sequence points. Baumeister et al (1994) clarifies with the example of a sexual response: "refraining from sex is undoubtedly much easier if one backs away after (or before) the first kiss than if one waits to intervene until after an hour of passionate necking" (p. 21). Clients should be helped to understand, however, that just because something is harder it is not necessarily also rendered impossible. Given the awareness of the proper incentive or dis-incentive (e.g. the Gun-Point hypothetical), a person regains the choice to disengage from the target behavior.

Summary: Freedom-to-Change is Ego-Syntonic

Phenomenologically, the outcome of this semi-didactic, semi-experiential Logotherapy designed to help clients appreciate that they are fundamentally free, and, thus, free to choose to change, is an ego-syntonic sense of liberation and a regained sense of being once again possibly in control of their lives. This realization that one is free to choose and free to change is so empowering that once clients are provided with a logical framework to counteract the notion of disease-based determinism, they tend to hold on to this insight. In this sense the realization of strategic freedom-to-change is much like learning to ride a bicycle: once understood, it requires no additional practice and it has no expiration date. It is quite a different story with the tactical, here-and-now awareness of choices available to us in any given moment: the habit of falling existentially asleep and living on a cognitive-behavioral auto-pilot has to be replaced by a habit of waking yourself up. That is the task of the second part of Choice Awareness Training that is discussed further below.

Chapter 5

Part II of Choice Awareness Training: Cultivating Tactical Freedom to Change

This part of Choice Awareness Training discusses the practice of tactical (here-and-now, ongoing) choice awareness and development of a daily Choice Awareness Practice as a way to potentiate change. The true challenge of Choice Awareness Training is not necessarily the task of helping the client awaken to their fundamental capacity to change but to help the client weave that realization into the very fabric of their life.

Choice Awareness Practice

The first part of Choice Awareness Training (facilitation of the strategic, philosophical, ontological appreciation for one's fundamental freedom to choose and to change) can be accomplished within four to six semi- didactic, semi-experiential sessions. The practice part of the Choice Awareness Training was an ongoing treatment modality that an inpatient substance use client availed himself of until the day of the discharge from the program.

As such, facilitated practice of choice awareness (through the attendance of the Choice Awareness Practice group and through corresponding choice-awareness clinical homework) is recommended as an ongoing programmatic element in structured drug and alcohol rehabilitation. The following is a discussion of how an initially Logotherapeutic intervention designed to facilitate the appreciation of the fundamental freedom-to-change transitions to a form of modified mindfulness practice designed to institute an appreciation of the here-and-now opportunities for choice as well as to facilitate an "installation" of a personal choice awareness practice habit.

Choice Awareness Practice Group Session Format

Choice Awareness Practice (CAP) was originally designed as a group modality (Somov & Somova, 2003), as part of an overall clinical curriculum of group-based modalities, such as motivation-leveraging Logotherapy group, "Meaning of Life" (Somov, 2007), Relapse Prevention Psychodrama (Somov, in press), and others. While the description of CAP below is customized to group setting, Choice Awareness Practice is just as well-suited for individual applications.

The CAP group, piloted in the correctional drug and alcohol treatment program, consisted of an ongoing discussion of the importance of developing a choice awareness routine interlaced with in-session practice of choice awareness that involve the practice choice awareness enhancing exercises.

Choice Awareness Practice Group sessions consist of four potential elements: a) ongoing review of the rationale of the choice awareness change variable and of its interplay with other aspects of recovery; b) assisting clients with initiating and fine-tuning their daily choice awareness practice; c) helping clients process the experiential fall-out/insights from their increased choice awareness; and d) providing clients with an in-session structured choice awareness experience both to raise their level of choice awareness and to model ideas for choice awareness applications and practices.

From Strategic Freedom to Change to Tactical Freedom

Having assisted clients with establishing their strategic awareness of their fundamental freedom to choose and change, facilitators begin to qualify the thesis of "you cannot not choose" by discussing various exceptions to this existential axiom. While the strategic sense of freedom-to-change is undermined by the client's all-or-nothing view of their self-control attempts, as well as by subscribing to the choice-disempowering Disease Model of addiction and choice-incompatible language, the tactical freedom to change is undermined by lack of choice awareness, i.e. by habitual, schematic, stimulus-response, unconscious, mindless responding to internal and external stimuli.

The overall goal of this section is to help clients realize that while they may be strategically free, they are not tactically free unless they are actively (or mindfully) aware of the choices imbedded in the here-and- now, particularly at various micro and macro crossroads of life.

Exploring the Barriers to Tactical Freedom

In exploring the barriers to Tactical (actionable, operational) Freedom, clients can be asked to ponder if there, in fact, some exceptions to the previously established existential maxim that "one cannot not choose." The following answers typically emerge, with minimal prompting:

We cannot not choose unless we are: a) dead (given particular beliefs about the after-life or absence thereof); b) comatose, unconscious, or asleep; and c) acting on an impulse, reflexively, automatically, mindlessly, in a scripted, pre-programmed, pre-rehearsed, rote, conditioned manner, out of habit, without the awareness of the choice options available in a given moment. This type of discussion of the barriers to the tactical, in- the-moment, here-and-now awareness of choices primes clients for the metaphor of conditioned, habitual, mindless behavior as a kind of sleep, and for the metaphor of choice awareness and mindfulness as a kind of awakening. The metaphor of mindlessness as sleep existentially upgrades the mandate of Choice Awareness Training to a goal of self-awakening from the lull of automaticity.

Tactical Choice Awareness Training & Gurdjieff-Type Mindfulness Training

Long after the days of the Buddha, the utility of here-and-now, tactical mindfulness would be echoed by many of

⟩hilosophical and psychological brokers of the East. Few came as close to a practical choice-awareness training system as Georgy Gurdjieff, a charismatic early 20th century Russian guru, nicknamed the "rascal sage" (Speeth, 1989). Gurdjieff likened an un-awakened human being to a machine, self (personality) to a collection of habits, and awakening or self- understanding to, at best, a lucid dream, or an awareness of being asleep. Gurdjieff did not believe that un-awakened human machines phenomenologically experience choice and denied the human machine a power of self-determination: "We have no capacity to do, no 'free will' – in fact, no function of will at all" (Speeth, 1989, p. 33). Gurdjieff posited that "Man is born, lives, dies, builds houses, writes books, not as he wants to, but as it happens. Everything happens. Man does not love, hate, desire – all this happens;" a person does not choose: "the situation chooses" (p. 33). But, according to Gurdjieff, the human machine can study itself, and can develop a capacity for true will (Speeth, 1989; Ouspensky, 1949). Gurdjieff emphasized self-study through self-monitoring of one's motor- behavioral and cognitive-affective habits. More specifically, he prescribed such de-automatizing activities as assuming and holding of an uncomfortable sitting or standing position, the use of non-dominant hands to perform various routinized tasks of daily living, and modification of one's writing. Thus, Gurdjieff taught freedom from automaticity. Langer (1989), the author of "Mindfulness," writing at the end of the twentieth century echoes Gurdjieff's early twentieth century formulations and recommendations: "the automatic behavior," she writes, "has much in common with habit" (p. 16) and notes that acknowledges that "proper meditation techniques are said to result in a state that has been called de- automatization" and in a state of freedom from stereotypes and rigid distinctions (p. 78; Langer's italics).

But Gurdjieff, of course, wasn't the only one to write about automaticity. Wells, as far back as 1927, in her work entitled "The Phenomenology of the Act of Choice," observes the so-called "habitual" choices: "with repetition the development of the processes entering into volitional consciousness tends quickly to become habitual." (p. 92). Wells preferred the term "habitual" choices are really a misnomer since they involve no consciousness per se and are nothing other than cognitive- behavioral defaults, or automaticity.

Wells, unlike Gurdjieff, apparently did not like the de-humanizing analogy to a machine, and felt that the term "habitual" choice, rather than the term "automatic," "better expresses the psychological constitution of the process" (p. 92). Barrett (1911) did not feel he had to be apologetic about the terminology of automaticity as he saw it not only normal but adaptive: "automatism is the natural issue of normal motivation... a manifestation of the protective economizing tendency of volitional functioning" (1911, p. 141).

Gurdjieff drew a distinction between people who experience events as if they "happen" to them and those who are free. This semantic distinction between people who "do" and people for whom "everything happens" is tantamount to a distinction between choice-ful-ness and choice-less-ness.

It should be noted that the practical part of the Choice Awareness Training proposed by Somov & Somova (2003) was inspired by Gurdjieff's teachings and can be reasonably construed as a form of modified mindfulness training the purpose of which is to increase a baseline of here-and-now awareness of choices, as an existentially-prophylactic catalyst of habit-modification.

Choice Awareness as Modified Mindfulness Training vs. Classic Mindfulness

While both Mindfulness and Choice Awareness Training are awareness training technologies, the two are somewhat different in focus. Mindfulness is awareness, "awareness of simply what is" (Dimidjian & Linehan, 2003). Choice Awareness is choice awareness, or awareness of the opportunity for a choice and of self as a Chooser behind the choices Buddhist mindfulness is an awareness of the external object with the purpose of assisting the meditator to eventually lose the sense of being an observer and to unite in the moment, with the moment, in a state of object-less, subject-less non-duality. Choice Awareness, by definition, is an awareness of choice, a meta-cognitive awareness of the fact that one has a choice (options at any given moment) and a capacity to choose. Therefore, choice awareness does not aim to blur the boundary between the subject and the object. On the contrary, it aims to reinforce one's sense of oneself as a subject, as a self-determining agency. Therefore while mindfulness meditation represents a period of non-judgmental observation passivity or non-doing, free of discursive, interpretive inner narrative, choice-awareness practice is an active process that infuses an awareness of choice into what was previously automated, characterized with discursive self-narrating of the options that one is tactically aware of and their alignment with one's strategic goals. Whereas mindfulness is a state of accepting willingness (Dimidian & Linehand, 2003), whereas choice awareness is a state of purposeful, psychologically healthy, and self-efficacious willfulness. In summary, mindfulness training is training in the awareness of being here-and-now, Choice Awareness Training is training in the here-and-now awareness of being free.

Demonstrating Automaticity, Mindlessness, and "Choice-less-ness"

The following are a few experiential ways to demonstrate automaticity, mindlessness, and "choice-less-ness" that can be used either as part of Choice Awareness Practice group or in the context of individual psychotherapy. Pointing Out the Here-and-Now Automaticity "Catch" clients in the middle of head nodding, leg shaking, and in the middle of their gestures. Point out the seeming mindlessness and automaticity of these motor behaviors. Help clients appreciate the fact that while they, in theory, had choices (about what leg to shake, how quickly to shake it, etc.), the behaviors "happened" on their own without their having been any conscious processing of the choice options or any conscious choosing. This type of immediate behavioral feedback is used to facilitate to a greater state of choice-awareness. As clients begin to become self-conscious, they, by definition, become conscious of their Selves: such moments of meta-cognitive self-awareness and self-observation afford an empowering glimpse of the dormant Chooser that is coming back "on-line."

Circle of Choice

Give clients four sheets of paper and have them draw a circle. Then, in rapid succession, have clients draw another one on a separate piece of paper, and another one on the last piece of paper. Following this, invite clients to comment on the similarities of these three circles ("In what ways are these circles similar?"). In most cases, the mindlessly drawn circles will reveal a range of similarities on the following parameters: clock-wise or counter-clock-wise direction of the circle, its diameter (large, small?), its relative position on the page (centered, up or below the center line?), and its starting point (twelve o'clock, three o'clock?). Ask clients if they consciously intended for these similarities to occur or if these similarities just happened. Ask clients to ponder what that means.

Following this discussion of mindlessness and automaticity, have clients draw a fourth circle, this time making conscious choices of where to start the circle, which direction to draw it, consciously choosing its diameter size and consciously choosing where to place it on the piece of paper. Have clients discuss how the experience of mindfully drawn circle differs from the previous experience of mindless drawing. Highlight any statements that indicate a sense of presence, a greater sense of control over the drawing. In discussing the experience of mindful circle-drawing some clients might convey a sense of being somehow alert, awakened, and attentive. Ask the semi-rhetorical question: "What if you could be this alert, this attentive and thoughtful at a baseline, with matters and events that have much impact on your life?"

The choice of a circle as a figure to highlight mindlessness is not a random one in this case, and the facilitator is encouraged to capitalize on the metaphorical and existential significance of a circle as a metaphor for mindlessness. After all, what makes a "vicious cycle" vicious is its circularity. Help clients appreciate that motor-behavioral and cognitive- affective habits are in essence circular stimulus-response patterns of "always doing the same thing without realizing it." Most substance use and compulsive spectrum clients readily relate to the phenomenological entrapment of being caught up in a repetitive cycle of doing the same thing over and over again, despite the sincere intent to break out of this behavioral loop.

Congratulating for Choices Made

As a means of highlighting the fleeting and subtle phenomenology of the actual act of choosing, the facilitator are encouraged to rely on their observation skills and congratulate clients for any apparent novel choices. Note that the emphasis in this technique is on the fact of a conscious choice rather than on its rationale. With this mind, clients are helped to transition from the perspective of content-based assessment of choices to a perspective of assessing the choice in terms of whether it was a true, conscious choice or a pseudo-choice, i.e. a stimulus-response reflex. Thus, the only "bad" choice is the choice that is not made.

Processing of the Meaning of the Word "Just"

While facilitators refrain from judging client's choices, they are encouraged to inquire about whether, in the client's own opinion, a given choice, if in fact consciously made, is in line with his or her treatment goals. Thus, clients are helped to appreciate the fact that a choice does not exist in a vacuum but is, in fact, indicative of the underlying motivations which maybe current and up-to-date or existentially out-dated.

Processing the meaning of the word "just" is one way to help clients learn not to confuse mindless actions with choice-based actions. Clinicians should be careful to make sure that this exercise is not experienced as a form of picking on the seemingly benign behavioral moments. To preempt the defensiveness, clinicians should introduce this clinical moment in explicit terms as a choice awareness exercise. For example, by asking a client's in a choice awareness practice group about the rationale for his or her sitting position in the room, you are likely to hear a defensive "just" of "I just decided to sit here." Patiently and non- reactively assist the client with the realization that by saying that he "just" sat there, he is, fact, saying that he sat in a given place for no particular reason and is, thus, in Gurdjieff's terms, claims that his behavior "just happened," without any conscious participation from him. Therefore, paraphrasing the word "just" as meaning "for no reason," the client is helped to appreciate the paradox of the moment: nothing happens without a reason and yet it somehow "just" did.

By inviting clients to unravel the mystery of clients' seemingly un-caused ("just happened") behavior, facilitators work to demonstrate how the behavior, even when not consciously chosen in the present, reflects possibly outdated motivation that might be in conflict with current recovery goals. These "just-s" can be also related to what Marlatt & Gordon (1985) referred to as "seemingly irrelevant decisions" that may lead to a lapse or a relapse. Consequently, clients are helped to see the potential role of choice awareness in relapse prevention.

The Arbitrary Choice: Practice of Spontaneity

If you were to be asked "What would you rather have: red or blue, one or one point three, a glass or a cup?" you would probably respond with a degree of annoyed bewilderment: "Red or blue what? One or one point three of what?! A glass or a cup of what?!" While this "offer" appears meaningless it is not without some choice awareness training value. Such offers represent the opportunity for a pure choice. If you were to be offered a $20 or $100 bill, "no strings attached," your choice would ore or less predetermined by the pragmatics of financial common sense.

Presenting a purely arbitrary choice, on the other hand, is challenge to common sense and pragmatics, and, as such, is a valuable opportunity to "wake up" and make a conscious choice.

In choice awareness practice, facilitators may offer clients meaningless choices that cannot be guided by the previously conceived considerations of pragmatics, commons sense, or value. Such un-motivated choices, in a way, represent what Tillich (1952) referred to as "freedom beyond freedom," an ultimate manifestation of spontaneity. A spontaneous choice is free the logic of the past. In its freedom from historical pre- determination, such choice has no past to rely on and, thus, can only rely on the here-and-now assessment of one's motivation, which requires presence and awareness. Evaluation of two equally meaningless options results in a choice of the purest kind. The capriciousness, subjectivity, irrationality, moodiness, unpredictability of such a choice highlights our freedom to choose in a manner that does not have to reflect our socio- economic, socio-cultural, and psycho-biological predispositions.

Who's Doing It?

The "Who's Doing it?" choice awareness exercise involves a simple task of repetitious execution of a motor behavior. For example, the facilitator may ask the client to clench his fist, but only after consciously choosing to do so. The facilitator tells the client: "clench your fist only after you have made a conscious choice to do so each and every time, and do that for a while." As the facilitator observes the client, he or she suggests that the client speed up the pace. Clients are likely to notice that they are able to increase the pace but they are not necessarily able to match the increased pace of the motor behavior with the pace of conscious choosing. In a manner of speaking, at a certain speed of behavior, they allow the behavior to begin to "happen" without consciously initiating it. Facilitators invite clients to process this experience in terms of their experience of choice and automaticity. Facilitators may also engage the client while the client is continuing with the exercise and ask: "Who's doing it? Who's clenching your fist while we are talking?" This demonstration of automaticity-on-demand is discussed in terms of our capacity to self-program, and, thus, self-reprogram, and its pro-recovery habit-formation value.

Thought Choice

In this exercise, participants are asked to repeat in their mind the word pronounced by the facilitator or to think the word opposite to the one pronounced by the facilitator. For example, as the facilitator says "black," clients will be, if choosing to accept the conditions of the exercise, choosing between "black" (same word) or "white" (opposite word).

With these instructions clarified, the facilitator begins to say the words "black" and "white" in random order, and continues to do so for a period of time (1-2 minutes). Following this facilitator stops the exercise and asks participants to share their experience. The theme to watch is the notion of trying to organize an otherwise chaotic stimulation. Some clients will report that after a few moments of stressful indecision they decided to always think the same word or to always think the word opposite to the one announced by the facilitator. The facilitator would do well to recognize this as a self-imposed autopilot that represents a trade- off between mindfulness and tension relief.

Following this discussion, the facilitator resumes several more mini- sessions of this kind, each time encouraging clients to choose freely on an ad-hoc basis, encouraging them to track the initial tension associated with ad-hoc choice and the temptation to initiate some kind of chaos-organizing autopilot.

In one such series the facilitator may choose one word, say, "black," and repeat it 20 times in a row, and process the participant's clinging to the arbitrary expectation of fairness and balance. In particular, some may note that they were waiting for the word "white" to balance out the "black." Discussion of how the client's expectation of somewhat intermittent sequencing of these words from the prior series is, too, an autopilot. Parallels with general expectations of fairness, balance, symmetry could be also discussed. Some clients may also report a sense of hopelessness or surrender, an increased temptation to switch to autopilot, be it "same" or "opposite," given the sameness of environmental stimulation.

Acceptance of "same" autopilot might be likened to surrender to peer/environmental pressure; while acceptance of "opposite" autopilot might be tentatively likened to oppositionality.

Finally, in the last presentation, the facilitator shall being with same black- white sequencing and then suddenly switch to north-south, right-wrong, left-right semantic dichotomies. Discussion of this will reveal the fact that clients – while trying to be awake in the sense of whether to "go same" or to "go opposite," – fell asleep in terms of potential variability of semantic dichotomies. Some will report the feeling of the inertia or momentum of the black-white semantic auto-pilot. The discussion of this semantic resistance, of this clinging to a familiar auto-pilot can be easily generalized to the dynamics of substance use.

Arbitrary Abstinence and Arbitrary Maintenance

Gurdjieff encouraged his students to give up "something valuable" but "not forever" in order to create a constant "friction between a 'yes' and a 'no'" (Ouspensky, 2000, p. 45). This suggestion offers a valuable choice awareness training opportunity as long as it is not misconstrued as an exercise in Stoic ascetism. Arbitrary Abstinence and Arbitrary Maintenance exercise is an opportunity for clients to practice both making choices (of what to quit and what to start), and serves to also hone their craving control skills for resisting temptations. In recommending this exercise as a choice awareness practice clients are emphatically encouraged:

a) to make only arbitrary choices about what to quit and what to start,

b) to commit to a pre-specified, time-limited abstinence or maintenance (timelines should be initially short and plausible, i.e. a week or a month); and

c) to feel free to break the commitment any time, if they

wish to do so, as long as this is done via a conscious choice.

Clients should be explicitly cautioned against misusing this exercise for dieting or going off medication and any other physiological parameters of their living that may jeopardize their health.

"I" Statement

Ask clients to attempt to mean the pronoun "I" each time they use it in speech. Engage them in a simple discussion and help them raise their awareness of whether they use the pronoun "I" by choice or mechanically, in mindless, un-free execution of speech autopilots. Suggest that clients may incorporate the "I" Statement technique into their daily speech as a choice awareness routine. Process the phenomenology of meaning the "I."

Uncomfortable Chair

This is an exercise that illustrates the choice in delaying gratification, an omnipresent problem for substance abusers. Participating clients are encouraged to assume a somewhat uncomfortable posture and become mindful of the discomfort and the desire to change posture. Doing so would create a sense of relief.

Process the choice in delaying the gratification of relief. Make parallels with substance use. Have clients re-engage in the exercise and experiment with the choice of the timing of the relief.

Choice Step By Step: Walking Meditation

Process mindlessness of walking, explore various choices of pace frequency, stride length, pronation, toe-first versus heel-first stepping, etc. Ask a client to choose each step. Suggest that actively choosing one step whenever one gets up from a chair or bed during the day might serve as a rather generalizable choice-awareness routine.

Crossing Arms

Ask participating clients to cross arms on their chest. Then ask them again. Process the habitual, automatic, mindless crossing (which arm goes over which arm). Highlight the mindlessness of habit.

Signature

Have clients sign their name, once or twice. Then have them sign it mindfully. Process how the mindful signature looks less valid because it is not automated enough. Discuss the benefits of mindlessness – such as signature authenticity; discuss drawbacks of mindlessness – such as the ease of signing whenever asked to sign, such as in the beginning of the exercise, and possibly jeopardizing one's privacy by making publicly accessible one's stamp of authenticity for possible replication.

The Choice to Let Go

The following choice awareness exercise provides a useful interface with anger management:

- Instruct the client to clench his/her fist and then ask him to open it.
- Ask the client to repeat this.
- Inquire about what, if anything, they have noticed.
- Comment on the fact that the way in which the individual opened his/her hand was (more likely than not) same across the two

hand-opening episodes.

- Identify this particular hand-opening behavior as an autopilot.
- Initiate the discussion of various choices available in opening of
the fist (the actual choice to open the fist, the timing of the release, the manner of the release (one finger at a time, sequence of the fingers, the whole hand, sudden vs. gradual opening, etc.)
- Create a metaphor of "letting go" by linking the clenching of the fist to tension and stress and facilitate a discussion of how, at times of stress, people tend to fall asleep by losing awareness of the freedom to let go, to release the tension.
- Ask clients to clench the fist again and provide metaphor- enhancing narrative along the lines of "You have a choice right now, you can stay tense or you can let go, if you decide to let go, you have a choice in how you will let go, go ahead a make a choice to either stay tense or to let go, if you decided to let go of tension, make a choice on how you will let go of it, all at once, or gradually, by holding on to your tension for a while..."
- Ask clients to repeat this but encourage them to make a different choice about how to let go.
- Repeat this several times, in succession, summarizing metaphorically the idea that not only do the clients have a choice to let go of tension, but that they also have a choice in how to let go of tension.
- Instruct clients to experiment with the timing of the release of the tension
- Instruct clients to allow themselves to use their other hand to open their clenched hand

The apparent value of the Choice to Let Go choice awareness exercise is that, if practiced on a regular basis, this choice awareness ritual:

a) In the spirit of progressive muscle relaxation, teaches clients to recognize bodily tension which they may use as a turning point at a moment of stress;

b) conditions the notion of freedom-to-change to psychophysiological relaxation and as such reinforces the idea that awareness of choices, at any given time frees one up, relieves one's tension about being trapped, or locked into a given internal or external circumstance; c) and re-conceptualizes tension, stress, and anger as a choice, a response option that does not have to be a default, as an affective autopilot that can be overridden.

The Choice to Let Go choice awareness exercise also yields to secondary metaphors. For example, asking clients to use their other hand to open the clenched fist may be metaphorically likened to seeking help or support. "Flipping the (proverbial) bird," by opening the fist with beginning with the middle finger, can be likened to displacement of anger, a tension- relieving, albeit less constructive, strategy for letting go of tension. Finally, continuing to clench the fist can be seen as a choice to hold on to the grudge or anger, and not wanting to release it.

In summary, the clinician may reiterate that tension or relief are but invisible choices if one is asleep. Consequently, regular practice of this exercise will allow clients to turn tension into a kind of choice awareness alarm clock that will awaken the person to the fact that he or she has a choice to stay tense or to let go.

The Choice Eye

The visual imagery, relaxation, and hypnosis literature make references to the metaphor of a "mind's eye." The present choice awareness practice involves the metaphor of a Choice Eye and, in format, vaguely follows Yapko's (2003) format for the Mind's Eye hypnotic induction technique.

More specifically, the client is instructed to close his eyes and imagine that he has a Choice Eye. This Choice Eye is likened to a physical eye, but inside one's mind. This Choice Eye sees automaticity, schematic behaviors, habits, and mindlessness. The client is instructed to let the eye roam, around and inside himself, in search of any behavioral autopilots or schemas, or habits, or mindlessly executed behaviors. Each time the

Choice Eye sees an autopilot, a mindlessly running behavioral or affective routine, it makes a choice. The Choice Eye chooses to continue to run the routine or to discontinue its operation for the moment. For example, the Choice Eye may see that the subject is tapping his or her foot. The Choice Eye then chooses to continue to tap the foot or to stop tapping it. And so and so forth. The person is instructed to perform this exercise for a few minutes, letting the Choice Eye take a panoramic view of the person's current moment.

A Different Way to Get 4

Write on a piece of paper the following and give it to the client: "___ + ___ = 4." Instruct the client to fill in the blanks. A typical response is, of course, " 2 + 2 = 4." Discuss that the "two plus two equals four" is an autopilot. Challenge the client to "get 4 a different way," and allow them to work on that problem for a couple of trials. The client may, for example, arrive at the following equations: "7 – 3 = 4," "569.5 – 565.5 = 4," "8 x 0.5 = 4," etc. State that if the client chose to, as of this moment, he could come up with a different way to obtain 4, each time, for the rest of his life, if this is all he did. Allow the client to ponder the infinity built into this simple algorithm.

Offer to the client to each day "find a new way to get four,' and make parallels with recovery. State that there's more than one way to get to Rome (more than one way to get 4). "Choosing another way to get what you want" and/or "appreciating that another way is possible makes for a good choice awareness practice.

Pattern Interruption

Facilitators may use a variety of pattern interruption elements to create opportunities for choice. For example, moving one's podium or easel in the group room to a new location allows clients to make a choice to adjust and to make a choice to regulate or not regulate any discomfort or inconvenience that a given pattern interruption might have created. Similarly, silence can be used to highlight clients' automatic preferences, such as a desire to break the tension of silence on group's behalf, to wait it out, hoping for someone else to do it on their behalf, etc. Clients may be asked to process the choices they had in the moment, and how they guided themselves through those choices. Similarly, Zeigarnik effect can be an effective method of pattern interruption to increase client's choice awareness. An example of a simple implementation of such pattern interruption strategy would be to start but not finish an utterance at any point of the choice awareness practice group.

Another variation on pattern interruption is starting a previously automated routine from an arbitrary point of entry. De Bono (1970) suggests that changing a choice of entry point may lead to insight. And indeed, if the choice of entry point is kept constant, the determinism of the behavioral algorithm leads to one and the same result. Einstein's definition of insanity (as doing one and the same thing but expecting a different result) illustrates the futility of mindlessness and automaticity quite well.

In working with substance use clients who have developed a habit of using the Serenity prayer, I have frequently recognized the philosophical/spiritual value of it, but also suggested a simple modification to turn this already recovery-oriented routine into a freedom- to- change potentiating choice awareness routine. In particular, I would instruct clients to each day make a conscious choice to start the Serenity prayer from a different point of entry. For example, a client could choose to start the prayer from word # 7. To accomplish this, he or she would have to first mindfully and mentally "walk through" the prayer structure to identify word # 7. Following this, the client would begin the Serenity prayer from an unusual point of entry. Quite often clients reported both enhanced choice awareness and state of wakefulness and a new appreciation of the actual text of the prayer. On occasion clients would discover new meaning possibilities. And almost always, clients would report a Zeigarnik like effect of needing closure after this pattern interruption. Knowing the lingering tension of the Zeigarnik effect, I would typically recommend that the clients choose not to redo the prayer but leave it as imperfect as it is, with the idea that this lack of closure from the pattern interruption would provide the lingering of an otherwise therapeutic meme. Several clients have confessed that they did, after all, "order" the sequence after some time of resisting to do so. My sense is that most, or at least the majority, of individuals in the state of lack of closure would at some point bring the pattern to completion. The therapeutic value here is obvious: in addition to choice awareness, the client is "tormented" with a benign and clinically meaningful obsession.

Get to Know Your Robot

One of the best correlates to Gurdjieff's method of de-automatizing that I have found in the self-help literature is the chapter "Get to Know Your Robot" in the book The Psychological War on Fat by Cordell and Giebler (1977). These authors provide a well-popularized discussion of automaticity and offer the readers to essentially catalogue their programs or habits. I have used a similar cataloguing technique in guiding my clients' choice awareness practice, by offering them to think of automaticity in terms of simple "if A, then B" algorithms that can be reprogrammed to read anything from "if A, then A" (viewing reality as is, through separation of Self into Subject and Object) to "if A, then (fill out the blank with a more adaptive alternative response)." It should be noted that the difference between Cordell and Giebler's use of the knowledge of one's robot is that they reprogram the robot through behavioral reinforcement, whereas the Change Equation reprograms the robot through choice or agency.

Pressing Flesh

In group setting, have two clients shake hands. Help them deconstruct the experience. Discuss the unintended, un-chosen communication imbedded in a street-style high-five handshake/hug. Explore the handshake as a link in the potentially long and treacherous chain of small-talk if in the presence of stimulus-laden people, places, and things. Have clients press flesh in a de-automatized, choice-aware fashion.

Demonstrating the Emotionally Pragmatic Appeal of Mindlessness and Automaticity

As part of Choice Awareness Training, the following "Word Choice" exercise can be used as both an opportunity to demonstrate the emotional pragmatism of choosing not to choose and as a choice-training exercise. Participants are instructed to repeat in their mind the word pronounced by the facilitator or to think the word opposite to the one pronounced by the facilitator. For example, as the facilitator says "black," clients will be saying to themselves the word "black" (same word choice) or "white" (opposite word choice). With these instructions clarified, the facilitator begins to say the words "black" and "white" in random order, and continues to do so for a period of one or two minutes.

Following the exercise, the facilitator offers to discuss the experience. The theme to highlight is clients' attempts of trying to organize an otherwise chaotic stream of stimulation. Some clients will report that after a few moments of repeated stressful indecision they decided to always think the same word or to always think the word opposite to the one announced by the facilitator. The clinician facilitates the discussion of this dynamic, of its existential meaning and its parallels with substance use. In particular, clients are helped to appreciate the freedom-escaping allure of the self-imposed autopilot that represents a trade-off between the stress of conscious, mindful choosing and tension relief.

Following such discussion, the facilitator encourages clients to "claim" their freedom to choose, to not go on auto-pilot, to choose freely on a moment-to-moment basis, and resumes the exercise. This "Word Choice" exercise can be used repeatedly as a choice-conditioning, with the term "conditioning" here being akin to muscle conditioning. Methods for self-administration of this choice-conditioning exercises (such as making a recording with a random presentation of these word stimuli or involving a support person to work with the client) can be discussed as well.

Emotional Deepening: The Costs of Automaticity

Mindless, reactive, habitual, mechanical, schematic, rote, conditioned, fixed, rule-governed, impulsive, stimulus-bound, auto-piloted existence is not unlike being asleep or sleep-walking, at best. This can be a rather existentially-poignant and, thus, motivationally-enhancing realization: most would be appalled at the notion of sleeping away their life. To deepen the appreciation for the need to be more awake and aware, clinicians can offer a kind of existential accounting to help clients ballpark how much conscious time they have actually lived (by factoring out actual nighttime sleep and conditioned sleep of mindlessness that pervades our lives). Pushing the existential button of time loss allows the facilitator to heighten clients' motivation for the need to wake up and to stay awake, if they are to live as themselves, prudently apportioning time, their only existential resource, to what, indeed, matters.

Daily Choice Awareness Habit: Setting an Alarm-Clock for the Mind to Awaken the Sleeper

By this point in Choice Awareness Training, clients realize that knowing the value of choice awareness does not make one choice-aware. An existential sleeper is asleep and is unaware of that fact and, short of outside help, will remain asleep. While counting on others to rouse oneself from cognitive-behavioral auto-pilots is certainly possible (through therapy and/or self-help meetings that remind one of his or her goals and priorities), learning to wake yourself up to the here-and-now freedom to choose and to change is the ultimate goal of Choice Awareness Training. Gurdjieff offered an elegant self-help solution for this problem. He believed that "it is possible to change certain aspects of overt behavior and to use such changes as reminders for flagging attention" (Speeth, 1989, p. 77). In particular, Gurdjieff suggested that an individual can set up a kind of mental alarm-clock that would awaken the individual continuously throughout life, at various selected time-points (Ouspensky, 1949).

Gurdjieff's suggestion, in the context of Choice Awareness Training, takes the form of cultivating a habit of de-constructing and consciously re-constructing various habits of daily living as an opportunity to infuse choice awareness into various routines of daily living. On a practical level, the client might begin with de-constructing their evening hygiene, re-sequencing its various steps, and including such "choice awareness twists" and mindfulness-raising alterations as brushing with a non-dominant hand, brushing and washing with one's eyes closed, making a conscious choice to not use the mirror on occasion, etc. For weeks, if not months, the client consciously varies his or her evening hygiene routine until he or she either tires of it or the new routine begins to feel old (i.e. too familiar to be of choice-awareness and mindfulness- facilitating value). At this point, the client makes a conscious choice to target a new daily habit. Once the client appears to have exhausted all available targets, he/she can recycle the previous targets. The opportunities for anchoring choice awareness in one's daily routines are practically limitless.

Helping Clients Select a Target for Daily Choice Awareness Practice

In selecting a choice awareness practice clients are encouraged to consider habits that are high in frequency and are likely to occur on any given day of a client's life regardless of circumstance and surroundings (such as hygiene routines, for example). Furthermore, it is recommended that clients try to anchor their choice awareness practice in high-frequency that are also reasonably paced throughout the day (e.g. mindful, choice-aware eating).

Portable Choice Awareness Practice

Conscious drawing of a circle (see more detailed explanation above) is recommended as a portable choice awareness practice that can help clients both internalize the metaphor of the self-reinforcing circularity of habits and provide an easy, on-the-go meditation on choice awareness.

Chapter 6

Recovery Autopilot

Not All Mindlessness is Bad: Pro-Recovery Automaticity

The discussion of the potential benefits of mindlessness and automaticity allows clients to develop a balanced view of the pros and cons of being on an auto-pilot. It is paramount that clients avoid the sweeping generalization that all automaticity is unhealthy. Habits are necessary and essential for adaptation.

Clients are helped to appreciate the utility of both change-facilitating and change-maintenance recovery habits. Clients are encouraged to recognize that by the very virtue of their participation in treatment they are choosing to "program" themselves to respond with a certain pro-recovery automaticity in the face of possible future challenges to their recovery goals.

With this in mind, later sessions of Choice Awareness Training, aside from concluding comments about choice awareness, is also an opportunity to integrate various skills clients are learning in the Program into a kind of "recovery habit."

Recovery Autopilot as a Maintenance Tool

While clients are encouraged to develop a Recovery Autopilot, facilitators clarify that the purpose of the autopilot is to help clients transition from a structured therapeutic environment to independent self-care.

With this in mind, the Recovery Autopilot is seen as a temporary measure to be used in the immediate post-treatment future. The Recovery Autopilot format can, however, eventually serve as a platform for client's general mental health hygiene and self-care.

Recovery Autopilot Exercise

Recovery Autopilot may be presented to clients graphically as a the following equation:

Recovery Autopilot = Daily Recovery Ritual + Weekly Recovery Event(s)

Facilitators explain that a recovery autopilot consists of a daily recovery ritual (which with time may become a platform for generic self-care) and a weekly recovery event.

Time Allotments

Let us assume that a client is willing to spend thirty minutes a day on a Daily Recovery Ritual and at least one additional hour per week on some kind of Weekly Recovery Event.

Daily Recovery Ritual Samples

It is recommended that a client spends this half-hour on a combination of Relaxation/Meditation, Self-Motivation, Social Support, Choice Awareness activity, Review of Program Materials or some Recovery- related Reading or Study. The following are a few sample breakdowns of what your Daily Recovery Ritual could be:

Recovery Autopilot Sample 1:
Cue-Conditioned Relaxation (5 min)
Practice Choice Awareness (5 min)
Analyze Recent Cravings (10 min)
Motivation Review: review your reasons for recovery (10 min)

Recovery Autopilot Sample 2:
Cue-Conditioned Relaxation (5 min)
Practice Choice Awareness (5 min)

Review Lapse Prevention Plan (10 min)
Perform a Relapse Prevention Hypothetical (10 min)
Recovery Autopilot Sample 3:
Cue-Conditioned Relaxation (5 min)
Practice Choice Awareness (5 min)
Listen to your Motivational Pitch Tape (10 min)
Plan Natural Highs for the coming up weekend (10 min)

It is recommended that any Daily Recovery Ritual should include a relaxation and a choice awareness practice; keeping these items constant assures that the client engages in a key use prevention skill and at least minimally "wakes" oneself up to his/her sense of freedom to change by becoming aware of choices available to him/her in a given moment. The remaining portion of the Daily Ritual may vary and relate to the rest of the Recovery Equation.

While the Daily Recovery Ritual may vary somewhat in term of its content, it is important, however, that the Daily Recovery Ritual follows a predictable pattern or system, time- and format-wise. After all, if it is too random, it would not be a ritual, would it?

Tips for Daily Recovery Ritual

Clients are encouraged to keep the Daily Recovery Ritual simple but meaningful. Clients would do well to resist the temptation to be too "recovery-greedy." More is not always better. Clients should keep the Daily Recovery Ritual realistic; a plan that is too tedious will feel like too much of a burden and will eventually collect dust Furthermore, clients are encouraged to come up with at least two versions of a Daily Recovery Ritual and plan to alternate them every other day. This way clients will be able to make use of most of what they have learned while keeping it interesting.

Weekly Recovery Events

In addition to a Daily Recovery Ritual, it would be a good idea for a client to also get in a habit of scheduling at least one hour worth of Recovery Events per week. The following is a list of potential ideas that may be provided to a client as a generic menu for them to pick and choose a Weekly Recovery Event on a regular basis.

- Volunteer or Charity event
- Natural High of client's choice (exercise, entertainment, etc.)
- Time alone
- Review of Recovery/Program Materials
- Self-Review: analysis of one's choices, cravings, recovery investments over past week
- Choice-Awareness Chess Match
- Therapy/Counseling Session
- Self-Help Meeting of one's choice
- Religious or Spiritual meeting/function

Chapter 7

Choice Awareness Check

The purpose of Choice Awareness Check Group is to allow treatment participants to consolidate their belief in their power of self-determination as well as to allow group participants to become inoculated to any arguments designed to undermine their sense of self-efficacy. Finally, the purpose of the group is to create a moment of accountability with a corresponding motivation-enhancing dissonance. The intended effect is to place a group participant in a situation in which he or she ardently defends his or her freedom and verbalizes the need for choice awareness, as a dissonance-inducing contrast for any unsystematic or inconsistent practice of choice awareness. In other words, as a group participant finds himself in a position to "preach" choice awareness, he feels compelled to at least attempt a systematic practice of the skill in question.

Additionally, Choice Awareness Check Group allows for vicarious learning and interpersonal feedback. Group participants are exposed to their fellow group members' "theses" on choice awareness and ideas about choice awareness practice – such excessive but idiosyncratic review of the material allows group members to further internalize the underlying clinical message by learning from their peers.

The duration of the group corresponds to the number of the group participants with each participant taking a single session to present his understanding of the need for choice awareness and his choice awareness practice routine. Following the introductory session, a list of clients' presentations is created and the clients are given a "choice awareness check" form to guide their preparation and presentation on their respective dates. Each session begins with a "presentation" and is followed by a Q & A session that is moderated by the group facilitator.

Chapter 8

Chess as a Choice Awareness Practice

Chess, as a game of strategy, is an excellent choice awareness game: it offers substance use clients a practice of ongoing evaluation of choices in terms of their consequences. Much of the behavior of substance use (and of the compulsive spectrum behavior) is tactical in its impulsivity, driven by short-term, immediate gratification. Chess teaches delayed gratification and, thus, impulse control. Chess, therefore, proves to be a viable anti-dote to tactically myopic compulsive functioning and prompts a player to evaluate the strategic ripple effects of any given choice.

Chess is also a rare interpersonal opportunity for silence and offers practice opportunities for emotional self-regulation of the emotions associated with victory or defeat. Finally, it is one of the few games that offers more than a binary/dichotomous outcome of win or lose. With its possible outcome of a tie, the game highlights the notion that not every form of competition is a zero sum game.

But above and beyond these already built-in choice-awareness and psychologically invaluable teaching moments, chess can be turned into a power-tool for choice awareness with a little bit of "tweaking." The following is a description of how chess was piloted as a choice-awareness enhancing tool in the context of the correctional/residential drug and alcohol treatment program. Upon admission, clients were provided with a brief overview of the choice awareness enhancing properties of chess and were, consequently, encouraged to learn to play chess. Chess, as a game of skill, was programmatically endorsed over such games of chance as cards. Regular chess tournaments were held each week with the first and second place winners earning various program privileges or nominal gifts, in proportion to the resources, policies, and logistics of the correctional setting.

Having assured that the majority of the program clients have learned to play chess, the program staff introduced a Choice Awareness Chess Tournament which involved an arbitrary change of board rules. For example, the knight and the bishop chess pieces exchanged functions. As a result, the players – who by now had arranged themselves in a natural hierarchy of regular chess competence – were essentially equated in their playing power. With the new set of rules, the most choice-aware player was the most likely one to win. As the clients progressed through the program, they continued to be presented, from time to time, with Choice Awareness Chess tournaments with ever-unpredictable arbitrary modifications to the rules of the game, with each tournament being conducted on a set of new board rules.

Choice-Awareness Chess Modifications

A variety of modifications to chess rules are possible. For example, it could be agreed, for the purposes of the Choice Awareness Chess tournament, that pawns are allowed to always move two squares, or that a pawn can take over a piece both diagonally and directly in front of it. Furthermore, contrary to the classic premium on time during chess tournaments, Choice Awareness Chess tournaments would set time minimums to encourage clients to play "slow chess" as yet another way of leveraging choice evaluation, impulse control and strategic thinking.

Choice-Awareness Chess Tournaments as a Follow-Up Intervention

Substance use programs may consider holding Choice Awareness Chess Tournaments as a form of clinical follow-up. Such events may be held on an ongoing basis and follow the format of a chess club. Such chess tournaments would be offered as a post-treatment self-help opportunity for the graduates and alumni of substance use treatment, and may be facilitated or autonomously run by former clients, with organizers surprise-announcing the modifications of the rules on the days of the tournament.

Chapter 9

Clients' Reactions to Choice Awareness Training

The Choice Awareness Training, as noted above, was initially designed as a part of a comprehensive substance use treatment curriculum and was subsequently applied in the context of a residential correctional substance use treatment program that took place in a program-devoted pod/cellblock of a county jail in Pittsburgh, Pennsylvania. No quantitative evaluation of this treatment modality has been yet undertaken. The following are a sample of client statements about Choice Awareness Training. These statements are taken from a weekly newsletter ("The Weekly Fix") issued by the inmates that participated in the program in question.

These reactions provide a touching glimpse into how these correctional substance use clients (most of whom had been previously exposed to the Disease Model of addiction and to the 12 Step programming) responded to the proposition that they are fundamentally free to choose and, thus, to change. It should be noted that the participation in the pilot program was not accompanied by any legal assistance in the form of early release or sentence reduction. It should be noted that The Weekly Fix was entirely produced by the inmate population and the program staff exercised absolutely no editorial control over this in-house initiative.

Inmate client J. K. (The Weekly Fix, Issue 1, at the beginning of the program pilot) reveals the paradigm clash: "I must say that the program here <...> is not at all what I expected. <...> I've been brought up being told that AA and NA were the only solutions for my drinking and drug using... The biggest difference leading me to problems is step one of NA... This step differs immensely from what is taught here. We have the power to choose to use or not... In retrospect I can see how my belief that I'm powerless is harmful to me. It was an easy way out. All responsibilities for the consequences of my using

<are> avoided by this simple belief. In all actuality these consequences are a direct result of an active choice I made to get high. Time will tell if I can adapt to this new way of thinking or not. I believe I can."

Inmate client H. T. (as early as in the second issue of the Weekly Fix) begins to zoom in on one of the core ideas of Choice Awareness Training. In his article "A Really Old Habit" H. T. reframed his substance use from a disease to a habit: "Most of my life, ever since I can remember, I have had the habit of biting my finger nails. <...> I am now 39 years of age, incarcerated for another habit, this one being potentially life threatening." So, the denial of having a disease of addiction without the denial of the detriment of one's habit of substance use can, in fact, co-exist!"

Inmate client K. W. (The Weekly Fix Issue 3) opens with an editorial entitled "Turning the Auto-Pilot Off:" "I believe the more aware you are, the better chance you have in recovery. Being aware of the smallest things can help: like how you dress, how you brush your teeth or how you tie your shoe laces can keep you from going back to sleep. <...> I've learned that when I am aware of my options, and take time out to weigh them, and see what fits for me, it seems to make it a better day. I'm not always going to make the right choices, but as long as I'm awake and aware, I can no longer be on auto-pilot or unaware of my actions." These thoughts are a clinical treasure trove.

In the same issue (The Weekly Fix 3), inmate client who anonymously runs the column "Fact or Fiction, by Someone,' challenges his peers: "Choice awareness practice keeps me switched off the auto-pilot. And makes me aware that there is a number of options available to me, and when I choose an option, it is chosen mindfully."

This "someone" is obviously no longer another anonymous statistic of powerlessness in the Alcoholics

Anonymous or Narcotics Anonymous, but a "somebody" aware of his power to choose and to change.

In the same issue (The Weekly Fix 3), **J. S. H.** announces the arrival of his agency with the following title: "I Have the Strength Within." He continues: "The power is within me. I realize that I can't look to others for 100% guaranteed support. <...> In recovery there might not be anyone there (for you) at all. In times of weakness, I need to search myself and then look to others." Note the wisdom: the client is sober that he can't solely rely on home groups, sponsors and support networks. His recovery is portable because it is based on his own strengths. Note that this is not reactive pouting to a lack of conjugal visit: the client is not dismissing others' help, but merely no longer willing to rely on it as an exoskeleton to carry his weight.

The former anonymous "Someone," now a "Somebody," per his pseudonym, albeit still anonymous, offers a unique take on the Choice Awareness Practice exercise in the Weekly Fix issue 4: he offers a game of "Dare and Catch Yourself." For example, "dare – to try and break an old habit, to not keep repeating the words "for real... for real;" and "catch yourself – tapping or humming, reacting over and over in the same way, asking question that have already been answered." This "somebody" is certainly showing some (creative) mind. Choice awareness, by virtue of opening up new options, has the effect of opening up the mind.

Speaking of opening the minds: **inmate client D. F.** (The Weekly Fix, issue 5) observes – "It's kind of funny how our minds work." He offers a choice awareness prank. Ask a peer: "How do you spell "silk?" Then, ask: What do cows drink? The usual response will be milk. Then you say: that's what people drink, cows drink water." D. F. is catching on to the vulnerability of mindlessness. His writing echoes a sentiment that was frequently noted by clients: they were quick to realize that stimulus-bound mindlessness is rife for exploitation.

The Weekly Fix, issue 8: an alpha-male **inmate client "G."** champions a full-on head-on with the notion of addiction being a disease. "I am glad to have the confirmation that I don't have a disease. For a long time I subscribed to the disease concept of addictions. This came from a lot of cognitive distortions I've picked up from attending N. A. and A. A. meetings. I am not doomed! <...> I am truly excited to learn that there is another way of staying clean. <...> The more I learn, the more it makes sense to me. A big part of my life, my decision making process has been to act on impulse <...> almost as if I had no choices. Rational recovery introduces me to phrases like "auto-pilot," "choice awareness," and "self- regulation," along with plans for lapse and relapse prevention, just to name a few. (This) gives me a "wonderful opportunity" to flex my "choice muscles." Come to think of it: this is all I ever wanted to do in the first place." This "testimony" speaks for itself. C. P. asks in The Weekly Fix (issue 11): "Have you chosen to be free?" The misleading simplicity of this question conceals this client's in-depth understanding of the issue at hand: freedom manifests through an act of conscious choice.

Inmate client D. F. (The Weekly Fix, issue 11), in a drawing entitled "Mind Garage," amidst the drawings of a bicycle, a lawnmower, a garden hose, and an oil spill, has thrown in a self-affirming pearl: a call out that reads "You are not a victim." D. F. carries the theme over to the next issue (The Weekly Fix, issue 12): in the same "mind garage," among the same objects, in the driveway, he writes: "Potential impact of the disease? Inescapable fate..." D. F., here, seems to be in the midst of spring cleaning of his "mind garage," getting rid of the clutter of the victim identity and the disease identity.
H. T. (The Weekly Fix, issue 13) proclaims: "Choice awareness expands our options. <...> I find that there are seemingly endless choices." Well said.

In the same issue, we learn of the identity of the anonymous "Someone" who began the rubric "Fact or

Myth." Having initially signed off as an anonymous "Someone," and having then progressed to a still anonymous "Somebody," he finally reveals his identity: he is N. M. In challenging his peers, he asks: "Choice awareness is all about being told what to do... Fact or myth?" We can safely guess his answer. What remains a mystery is the progression from anonymity to reclaiming one's identity: could it be the effect of a humanistic treatment approach? One thing is for sure: N. M. took the responsibility for his penmanship. Nobody told him what to do...

D. F. (the "Mind Garage" author, in the issue 14 of The Weekly Fix) offers a very cogent insight: in an article, entitled "Preset Recovery," he writes: " I was listening to my radio the other day trying to find a song <...> and realized how used to the pre-set channels I was. So I figured: what a wonderful opportunity to practice my Choice Awareness, so I changed the pre-set stations. <...> Each and every day I am getting closer to not living a pre-set life." D. F.'s essay is a glimpse into a mind free of pre-set recovery dogma.

Issue 5 of The Weekly Fix has a telling and humorous cover element. You see the following text encased in a rectangle: "I made a choice to put a rectangle around these words."

Issue 16 features clear thinking from **J. F.**: "Some things are not comfortable when not run on an auto-pilot. <...> But with pain, there's gain. I need to exercise my choice muscles which make me mindful so that I don't limit myself with mindless decisions. <...> When you take the time to consciously look around at everything around you, there are many options and life is limitless." J. F., who also signs off on this article as the "3d Eye" has his vision back.

D. F. (in The Weekly Fix issue 16) shows the readers his new acquisition for his "Mind Garage:" "It helps to be willing to change." Indeed.

M. H., in the same issue, shares: "When I come to jail I just get into the mix of things. <...> Then I get out and go right back to the same thing. It just becomes a cycle of using and coming back to jail. <...> This time I make a choice to use this time mindfully. <...> I know something is different this time. That something is me." M. H. here speaks of the revolving door of incarceration, but he might as well be speaking of the revolving door of the kind of recovery that takes the agent of change out of the equation of change. After all, what use would there be for M. H. in the equation of disease?

The editors of The Weekly Fix devoted the 21st issue to Choice Awareness Practice (which in the program was known by the acronym C. A. P.). The cover features a ferocious baseball cap, the bill of which is drawn in a manner of tooth-ful scowl. The text above the C. A. P. reads: "Put On a Mean Cap." The text below deciphers the in-house acronym: "Choice Awareness Practice – mornings, evenings, afternoon, nights."

Jumping ahead to the 32nd issue, we see the following thoughts by T. G.: "When I first heard about auto-pilots, the idea was to break them. By breaking them I slowly began to wake myself up. I found a lot of good out of becoming the thinker behind the thought. <...> I feel that this is going to be the one most important thing to keep me on top of my recovery."

Inmate client M. S., writing in the same (32nd) issue notes: "Before I never thought I had options <...> because I was in a deep sleep. I lived most of my adult life absent from my thoughts. <...> I have learned how to switch off my auto-pilot by doing two or three five minute choice awareness practices a day. It (practice) lets me be more aware and awake. <...> When I do some simple C. A. P. (Choice Awareness Practice), it lets me know that I am my own agent of change and that my life is up to me."

In reviewing the last, 33d issue of The Weekly Fix, at the very back of the issue we find an anonymous vignette entitled "Recovered or Recovering." The very phrasing of this item highlights an awareness of an option that for most of the participating clients did not phenomenologically exist. Choice Awareness Training is designed to help clients recover their sense of control, and with it their prognosis of recovery.

Chapter 10

Concluding Statement

Choice Awareness Training, as an existential-experiential (Logotherapy/Mindfulness Training) approach to substance use and compulsive spectrum presentations, is offered from the operating platform of Positive psychology, namely, from the position of capitalizing on free will as a fundamental treatment asset, and in contrast with the view of addiction as a disease.

The author proposes a view of addiction as a process in which the initially conscious choice to engage in an appetitive behavior becomes a habit. The author posits that in order to reverse the process of addiction, clients should be assisted with:

> a) modifying freedom-restricting cognitive schemas (e.g. disease model of addiction) and
> b) re-infusing choice awareness into their otherwise automated, mindless, stimulus-bound, compulsive, reflexive, reactive, unconscious, choice-unaware, habitual behavior.

Appendices (I – VI)

The following appendices (I – VI) are several alternative ways of phrasing an introduction to CAT and its key exercises.

Appendix I

CAT Intro: Choice Awareness Training

Freedom manifests through the *awareness of a choice*.
But what is a *choice*? We say we "have a choice" when
we are aware of options *to select* from. Thus, the notion
of "choice" refers to:

> a) the awareness of the options available, and

> b) the act of selection of one of the options.

Becoming aware of the options restores our sense of
freedom, takes us off the auto-pilot, off the zombie mode,
and gives us an opportunity to change our patterns,
habits, rituals, routines.

Theoretical Freedom

We are fundamentally free. And yet, in our everyday life,
we do not feel free. We mindlessly repeat the same
patterns over and over, and, as a result, end up feeling
caught up in a vicious cycle of sameness, feeling
powerless to change. This kind of mindlessness, this
sense of being stuck, is true of all of us, and
is particularly true of compulsives (such as perfectionists,
substance users, etc.).

Operational Freedom

Operational (or practical, actionable) freedom is
proportionate to our mindfulness, i.e. to our presence in
the moment, to our awareness of the options available to
us at any given moment. The more options we are aware
of at any given moment, *the freer* we are.

Increasing Operational Freedom

When you are stuck in a "should," when you are mindless, when you are flying blind on an autopilot of a given habit, you don't see any options other than the course of action that is expected of you. Your operational freedom is close to zero. You are a zombie, a robot, a passenger of what's been programmed into you. Acceptable alternatives, of course, exist but you are not in a habit of looking for them.

The goal of Choice Awareness Training is to increase operational freedom by looking for the alternatives and by practicing the psychomechanics of choice. Ultimately, the goal of Choice Awareness Training is to de-program the zombie so that he/she can consciously re-program oneself, in order to own one's life rather than to keep living out someone else's expectations.

Appendix II

Choice Awareness Exercise: Make a Choice When It Doesn't Matter

If I offer you a $20 bill or a $100 bill and ask you to choose, the choice is more or less predetermined by the pragmatics: as such, it's not really a choice. Now, what would you rather have: a red or a blue, one or one point three, a glass or a cup? This offer seems meaningless. And it is. Meaningless offers, however, represent the opportunity for a *pure choice*.

So, when someone asks "What do you want to do?" and you have no preference, instead of copping out and saying "I don't care, you decide," I recommend that you decide. Make a choice when the actual choice doesn't matter to you.

Practice making a choice when it doesn't matter so that you can make a choice when it does.

Appendix III

CAT Exercise: Open Your Hand to Open Your Mind

Choice Awareness Training is designed to leverage a greater sense of freedom-to-change, to awaken the living zombie, to facilitate change-process.

Clench your fist, open it.

Clench it again, open it again.

Clench it one more time, open it one more time.

See the mindlessness and sameness of the pattern?

Now...

Clench your hand and open it *with conscious awareness* of the options available to you as a daily meditation. Try it a few times, each time choosing how you open the fist, infusing a dose of mindfulness into the moment.

Practice opening your hand to open your mind to the options available to you in the moment.

Also, if you find yourself tensing up and clenching your fists (say, in perfectionistic frustration), mindfully open your hand to both release the stress and to open your mind.

Appendix IV

Pattern Interruption: Waking Up the Zombie

George Gurdjieff, an early 20th century Greek-Armenian mystic, the pioneer of the so-called Fourth Way, prescribed *pattern interruption* activities (such as the use of non-dominant hands to perform various routine tasks of daily living) to wake up the human spontaneity from its slumber. Pattern interruption is one of the elements of choice-awareness training. Here's one of the pattern-interruption exercises that I developed for my clients.

Here's one of the pattern-interruption exercises that I developed for my clients. I have first described this exercise in 2004 in "Recovery Equation" and have since modified and tuned it. Here's how this exercise appears in "Present Perfect." The following is an *induction* version. I will post the *practice* version of this exercise in a later post.

The Circle of Choice (Induction Version)

Instructions:

1) Take three sheets of paper and a pen.

2) Draw a circle on each paper, for a total of three circles.

Note: please, do not continue reading any further until you have followed the steps above.

Look at these circles and note your first impressions of them as a group. What stands out for you? First, jot down your thoughts, then keep reading.

You are likely to notice the differences between the circles, first. That's your dichotomous, dualistic perceptual lens coming into play. We are programmed to perceive *differences* more so than *similarities*. This "difference filter" tends to first bring into focus how "this" circle is "not quite perfect" or how it's "off center."

Let us now notice the similarities: chances are that the placement of the circles on each page is similar. I bet all three circles are somewhat similar in diameter. Most likely, they are similar in the starting point (probably, between 12 p.m. and 3 p.m.) and all three circles are probably drawn in the same direction. If so, what do you make of these points of similarity? Did you *consciously* intend for these circles to be similar?

I am about to say something bizarre: *you did not draw these circles*. These circles, as evidenced by their unintentional similarities, have been drawn too mindlessly, too reflexively, too reactively, too mechanically, too compulsively, too robotically, too reactively, i.e. too unconsciously for you to take the credit for this action. This was a re-action, i.e. a re-enactment of some circle-drawing habit in your mind, not an action, since a true action involves conscious deliberation.

Now, I invite you to draw another circle but mindfully, with the awareness of the choice-options available to you. Consciously make the choices that you had not made the first time: *choose* where on the page to place the circle, *choose* the starting point, *choose* the direction in which you will draw the circle, *choose* the diameter of the circle, and *choose* whether to bring the ends of the line together to make a full circle or not. Go ahead.

How was the experience of drawing this last circle different from the experience of drawing the first three circles? What are the different choices that you made? Or did you make the same choices as before but you actually *made* them this time? Was this last circle drawn by you or did it just happen the way it did?

Perhaps this time you felt that you were "actually" present.

Congratulations: this time you *did* draw this circle.

Appendix V

CAT: Enso – Choice Awareness Calligraphy

Jung wrote: "It is not that something different is seen, but that one sees differently" (1958, p. 546). *Enso* is "zen" for "moon circle." The moon circle, in Zen Buddhism, is a symbol of enlightenment and is a frequent subject of calligraphy (Austin, 2001).

"In the hand of the enlightened person, brush-work transforms into brush-*play*" (p. 577). I invite you to practice choice awareness calligraphy. Try drawing a circle with one "easy sweep."

Unlike in the circle-drawing exercises, *choose not to choose*. That too is a choice.

Make one "easy sweep" and *accept the outcome* of your calligraphy for what it is, regardless of whether your *enso* is full moon or half-moon.

Appendix VI

CAT: Nakama - Encircle Yourself With Awareness

Choice Awareness Training is designed to leverage a greater sense of freedom-to-change, to awaken the living zombie, to facilitate change-process.

The Circle of Choice – Practice Version

Draw at least one mindful circle every day. Slow down enough to consciously take in all the options available to you at the moment: the hand you'll draw it with, the placement of the drawing on the page, the starting point, the direction, the diameter, whether you will bring the ends of the line together or not. Use this exercise as an alarm clock for your mind. Time this exercise strategically, before the events in your daily life that are fraught with compulsive mindlessness.

For example, if you tend to find yourself on the defensive during business meetings, right before you go in or when at the actual meeting, "doodle" a circle, mindfully, consciously. Allow this moment be a metaphorical reminder that this time you will not do what you usually do, you will go a different route: you will not defend, you will explain instead, if asked; instead of anxiously volunteering pre-emptive justifications, you will calmly wait to be asked and if asked about your course of action or your performance or your opinion on a given matter, you will explain (rather than defend) or share (without any unnecessary self-deprecatory qualifiers).

Here's another example: say, you have a bit of road rage. As you get into your car, before you put into gear, before you pull out of your parking spot, draw a mindful circle to wake yourself up to the interpretive options at your disposal. Sure, you can think as before, that everybody's stupid, or you can remind yourself of the option to recognize that everybody's doing the best that they can: if they could be - *at this moment in time* - any more attentive, organized, skilled in their driving, then they would be.

In short, as you use this choice-awareness meditation, keep asking yourself: what are the vicious circles that I am stuck in? What are the loops of my mindlessness? And as you identify them, time your choice-awareness circle-drawing meditation at critical times to awaken yourself to an alternative interpretation of what is.

Encircle yourself within the field of self-supportive choice awareness. And, of course, enclose others within your field of compassionate awareness. Choose to share your choice-awareness know-how within your *nakama** (with those who are within your inner circle of significance).

*Nakama: Japanese for "circle of friends"

About the Author

Pavel Somov, Ph.D. is a licensed psychologist in private practice in Pittsburgh, PA (USA). He is the author of 7 mindfulness-based self-help books. Several of his books have been translated into Chinese, Dutch & Portuguese. Somov is on the Advisory Board for the Mindfulness Project (London, UK). Somov has also published peer-reviewed articles on the use of psychodrama and logotherapy in the context of substance use therapy.

A recent, randomized study—published by *Mindfulness Journal*—shows that *Present Perfect* is effective as a standalone intervention. The study found that those who had read the book experienced a statistically significant reduction of self-criticalness, a result that was still maintained at a six weeks follow-up (Wimberley, Mintz, & Suh, *Mindfulness*, Nov. 2015).

Somov grew up in the Soviet Union and after serving in the Soviet military he immigrated to US in 1991.

Somov's book website is www.pavelsomov.com and his practice website is www.drsomov.com

Somov's Bibliography

Mindful Emotional Eating (PESI, 2014): Mindfulness Skills to Control Cravings, Eat in Moderation, and Optimize Coping

Anger Management Jumpstart: a 4-Session Mindfulness Path to Compassion and Change (PESI/PPM, 2013)

Reinventing the Meal: How Mindfulness Can Help You Slow Down, Savor the Moment, and Reconnect with the Ritual of Eating (New Harbinger, 2012)

Smoke-Free Smoke Break (New Harbinger, 2011). Somov, P.G., Somova, M. J.

The Lotus Effect: Shedding Suffering and Rediscovering the Essential Self (New Harbinger). Somov, P.G. (November 2010)

Present Perfect: From Mindless Pursuit of What Should Be to Mindful Acceptance of What Is (New Harbinger, 2010). Somov, P.G. (June 2010)

Eating the Moment: 141 Mindful Practices to Overcome Overeating, One Meal at a Time. In stores November 2008, New Harbinger Publications. Somov, P. G. (2008)

Recovery Equation: Motivational Enhancement, Choice Awareness, Use Prevention: an Innovative Clinical Curriculum for Substance Use Treatment. Somov, P.G. & Somova, M. J. (2003)

References

Abramson, L. Y., Seligman, M. E. P., & Teasdale, J. D. (1978). Learned helplessness in humans: critique and reformulation. Journal of Abnormal Psychology, 87, 49-74.

Bandura, A. (1977). Self-efficacy: toward a unifying theory of behavioral change. Psychological Review, 84, 191-215.

Barrett, B. E. (1911). Motive force and motivation tracks. Longmans: Green & Company.

Dimidjian, S. & Linehan M. M. (2003). Mindfulness practice. In O'Donohue, W., Fisher, J.E., & Hayes, S.C. (Eds.). Cognitive behavior therapy. (pp. 229-237). Hoboken, NJ: John Wiley & Sons, Inc.

Frankl, V. (1969). Will to meaning: foundations and applications of logotherapy. New York: The World Publishing Co.

Jellinek, E. M. (1972). The disease concept of alcoholism. New Haven, CT: College and University Press

Klingemann, H. et al. (2001). Promoting self-change from problem substance use: practical implications for policy, prevention, and treatment. Dordrecht, the Netherlands: Kluwer Academic Publishers.

Langer, E. J. (1989). Mindfulness. Perseus Books, Cambridge, MA.

Llinas, R. R. (2001). I of the vortex: from neurons to self. Cambridge, MA: The MIT Press.

Lonergan, B. J. F. (1957). Insight: a study of human understanding. London: Longmans, Green & Company..

Marlatt, G.A., & Gordon, J.R. (Eds.) (1985). Relapse prevention. New York: Guilford Press.

Miller, W. R., & Rollnick, S. (1991). Motivational interviewing: preparing people to change addictive behavior. New York: the Guilford Press.

Molina, F. (1962). Existentialism as philosophy. Prentice-Hall, Inc. Englewood Cliffs, NJ.

Ouspensky, P.D. (1949). In search of the Miraculous. New York: Harcourt, Brace, & Co.

Ouspensky, P.D. (2000). In search of the Miraculous. Moscow: Fair Press

Peele, S. (1989). Diseasing of America: How we allowed recovery zealots and the treatment industry to convince us we are out of control. Jossey- Bass Publishers, San Francisco, CA.

Prochaska, J. O. & DiClemente, C. C. (1986). Toward a comprehensive model of change. In W. R. Miller & N. Heather (Eds.), Treating addictive behaviors: Processes of change (pp. 3-27). New York: Plenum Press.

Satterfield, J. (2000). Optimism, culture, and history: the roles of explanatory style, integrative complexity, and pessimistic rumination. In J. E. Gillham (Ed.), The Science of Optimism & Hope, Research Essays in Honor of Martin E. P. Seligman (pp. 349-378). Radnor, PA: Templeton Foundation Press.

Saunders, B., Wilkinson, C., & Allsop, S. (1991). Motivational intervention with heroin users attending a methadone clinic. In Miller, W. R. & Rollnick, S. (Eds). Motivational interviewing: preparing people to change addictive behavior. (pp.279 – 292). New York: the Guilford Press.

Somov, P. G., & Somova, M. J. (2003). Recovery equation: Motivational enhancement/choice awareness/use prevention: An innovative clinical curriculum for substance use treatment. Imprint Books.

Somov, P. G. (2007). Meaning of life group: Group application of Logotherapy for substance use treatment. The Journal for Specialists in Group Work, 32 (4), 316-345.

Somov, P. G. (in press). A psychodrama group for substance use prevention training. The Arts in Psychotherapy.

Schaler, J. A. (1999). Addiction is a choice. Open Court.

Speeth, K. R. (1989). The Gurdjieff work. New York: Jeremy P. Tarcher/Putnam

Tengan, A. (1999). Search for meaning as basic human motivation: a critical examination of Viktor Emil Frankl's logotherapeutic concept of man. Frankfurt am Main: Peter Lang.

Tillich, P. (1952). The courage to be. Clinton, MA: Yale University Press.

Walters, G. D. (1999). The addiction concept: Working hypothesis or self-fulfilling prophecy? Allyn & Bacon, Needham Heights, MA.

Wells, H. M. (1927). The phenomenology of acts of choice: An analysis of volitional consciousness. Cambridge University Press, London.

Wilshire, B. (1998). Wild hunger: The primal roots of modern addiction. Rowman & Littlefield Publishers, Inc., Lanham, MD.

Wheeles, A. (1958). The quest for identity: The decline of the superego and what is happening to American character as a result. W. W. Norton & Company, Inc. New York, NY.

Made in the USA
Coppell, TX
02 December 2019

12239529R00059